The Architecture of Frank Gehry

"Being accepted isn't everything."

F.O.G., December 1984

The Architecture of Frank Gehry is published on the occasion of an exhibition of the architect's major works, 1964 through 1986, organized by Walker Art Center.

The Architecture of Frank Gehry

Foreword by
Henry N. Cobb

Essays by
Rosemarie Haag Bletter
Coosje van Bruggen
Mildred Friedman
Joseph Giovannini
Thomas S. Hines
Pilar Viladas

Commentaries by
Frank Gehry

Major funding for the exhibition was provided by the Jay Chiat Foundation, the National Endowment for the Arts, Museum and Design Arts Programs, Herman Miller Inc., and the Graham Foundation for Advanced Studies in the Fine Arts.

Additional support came from The Gerard Junior Foundation and The Rouse Company.

Presentation of the exhibition in Minneapolis was made possible in part by The Bush Foundation, the Dayton Hudson Foundation, the General Mills Foundation, The McKnight Foundation and the Minnesota State Arts Board.

First published in the United States of America in 1986 by Rizzoli International Publications, Inc., 597 Fifth Avenue, New York, NY 10017

ISBN Hardcover 0-8478-0741-X ISBN Paperback 0-8478-0763-0 LC 86-42730

Designed by Lorraine Ferguson. Printed and bound in Italy.

All schematic drawings and sketches reproduced in this book are by the architect, unless otherwise noted. Dimensions of drawings are in inches; height precedes width. Working and presentation drawings are courtesy Frank O. Gehry and Associates.

The architect's commentaries appear in bold-faced type.

(cover)
California Aerospace Museum   1982-1984
Los Angeles, California

View of the south facade of the museum with Los Angeles's downtown skyline seen in the distance, a skyline as distinct from the context of greater Los Angeles as it is from the architecture of Frank Gehry.

(frontispiece)
Loyola Law School
1981-1984
Los Angeles, California

Entrance from Olympic Boulevard on the campus's south side, with, from left: the Fritz B. Burns Building, the chapel, Merrifield Hall and South Instructional Hall.

Cover and frontispiece photos by Michael Moran.

Contents

With commentaries by
Frank Gehry

Selected Projects of Frank O. Gehry and Associates

Henry N. Cobb

Foreword

Architecture is an art of indirection: that is to say the architect does not make the building, but rather makes an elaborate set of instructions that direct the work of many others who actually make the building. Hence works of architecture are of necessity institutionalized, not just in the purposes they serve, but equally in the mode of their production. For between the architect's intention and the realization of his building a multitude of institutional mechanisms intervene—of finance, of law, of industry, of trade—that inexorably shape, encrust, encumber and too often suffocate both the process and the product of his art.

It is the notable achievement of Frank Gehry to have transcended, without rejecting, this institutional condition of architecture. Marvelously, and inimitably, he has managed to infuse his buildings with those qualities of immediacy, spontaneity and improvisational gusto that we customarily encounter only in works of art that have come directly from the hand of the artist. This no doubt explains why Gehry is so often characterized by admirers as an "artist," but it also suggests why he himself, with justifiable vehemence, correctly insists, "I'm an architect." For the true measure of his achievement resides in the fact that he works not outside but firmly within the normative framework of institutional constraints and procedures that define the contemporary profession of architecture. And it is precisely this passionate and simultaneous commitment to the seemingly irreconcilable roles of "artist" and "professional" that has given his work its distinctive poignancy and power.

In support of this judgment, a single example may be cited as emblematic. At Gehry's Loyola Law School campus, an ochre-colored exterior wall of splendid sobriety forms the background for three open stairways that burst exuberantly out of the upper floors and dance their way down to the courtyard below. Two of these stairways—one at each end of the building—twist and turn with such irrepressible abandon as to seem utterly and blissfully liberated from any constraints of economy, engineering or function. Yet these lyrical constructions in painted steel are by no means superfluous to the mundane workings of the building. In fact, they constitute a highly efficient primary circulation system, employing the humblest of materials to facilitate the movement of people from floor to floor. But that is not all: beyond this ingenious joining of the carefree to the purposeful, these exhilarating stairways, when seen together with the rigorously ordered openings in the wall from which they spring, offer the building's users an eloquent metaphorical speculation on the complex and ever-problematic relationship between freedom of action and the rule of law in human society.

At Loyola, as in a number of his best works, Frank Gehry has performed with consummate artistry the ultimate task of the architect. He has shown us how a work of architecture, having satisfied all requirements of use and technique, may yet illuminate and give meaning to the human condition while giving shape to the physical world.

Thomas S. Hines

Heavy Metal
The Education of F.O.G.

On 28 February 1984, on the significant occasion of his fifty-fifth birthday, even Frank Gehry admitted there was something to celebrate. Frequently depressed by perceived past "failures" and, by his own admission, "paranoid" about the future, Gehry could not deny that for the last ten years, his stock and his star had been steadily rising. For as he and the world entered the Orwellian year, Gehry had indeed achieved fame, notoriety and international prominence as one of the era's most provocative and creative architects.

Increasingly euphoric critical acclaim, coupled with numerous professional awards, was heightened by the announcement from the Walker Art Center of a Gehry retrospective to open in Minneapolis in 1986 and to travel subsequently around the country. Sustained by a wife and two young sons, by two older daughters from a previous marriage, and by a close relationship with his mother and sister, the relative happiness of Gehry's personal life echoed the professional success.

Meanwhile, his architecture, in its powerful, brutal, ugly-beautiful way, continued to reflect the pain, anger, tensions and ambivalences of his life and times. In his fifty-fifth year he was certain that the shaping forces upon his work had been his growing awareness of his "Jewishness;" his immersion in the world of art and his close identity with painters and sculptors; his lifelong obsession with textures and materials; his fascination with "low life" and the detritus of urban civilization; and finally, the influence, as in most human achievements, of family, friends and benefactors.

Painfully related to his increasingly conscious sense of Jewishness was the later-regretted act, committed in his twenties, of changing his and his family's surname from Goldberg to the "less Jewish" Gehry. At fifty-five, it still seemed to him to have been a mistake. Frequently over the years he had thought of changing it back. Yet, by 1984, he

The architect as "Frankie P. Toronto," in *Il Corso del Coltello,* a performance organized in collaboration with Germano Celant, Claes Oldenburg and Coosje van Bruggen, Venice, Italy, September 1985.

had been "Gehry" longer than he had ever been "Goldberg." Since his professional achievement was identified with the name Gehry, it was unrealistic to consider changing it again. But "in my gut," he confessed ruefully, the "Goldberg" element was still very strong.

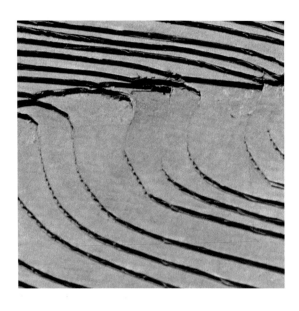

He was born 28 February 1929 in Toronto, Canada to Irving and Thelma Caplan Goldberg. His mother and his maternal grandparents had the greatest impact on his early development. Sam and Leah Caplanski had emigrated in 1908 with their four-year-old daughter Thelma and three-year-old son Kalman, from Lodz, Poland, where the talented, strong-willed Leah had worked as a "foreman" in her father's iron foundry. In Toronto, they simplified Caplanski to Caplan and slowly assimilated into their New World environment. In certain crucial ways, however, they retained Old World values, particularly religious ones. Sam was president of his synagogue, a small, remodeled houselike building, his grandson later recalled, similar, in some ways, to the house in Santa Monica that he, himself, would remodel in the 1970s. "My house reminds me of that old building," Gehry confessed, "and I frequently think of it when I'm here."

Both Caplans were politically leftist, coming from families that had devoted considerable time to union organizing. But Sam was foremost a Talmudic scholar, and he and Frank took long periodic walks together discussing Judaism and its implications for their lives. Frank attended Hebrew school and spoke with his grandparents in Yiddish. His Jewish name was Ephraim.

Equal in importance to his grandfather's spiritual and political guidance was the fact that he also owned a hardware store, where between the ages of ten and seventeen, the grandson had a part-time job. Stocking the store's shelves with the usual hardware inventory of nails, screws, bolts, hammers, saws, pliers, pipe, chains, fencing, roofing, paint and glass, young Frank acquired his lifelong fascination with "the nature of materials," an interest that would strongly affect his work. The store also had an appliance repair department with a changing display of radios in surgery and a gasoline pump out on the sidewalk where Frank dispensed gas to Toronto motorists.

Grandmother Caplan had not only a strong visual sense but a knack for fun and play as well. From the floor of the store's "fixit department," she and her young grandson would gather scraps and shavings from the lathe and take them home to the living room floor as the raw material for futuristic cities and giant connecting causeways. Later in Los Angeles, in his depressed early twenties, while driving a truck, attending night school and thinking about what he "wanted to be," he recalled scanning his past for clues. The hardware store and the cities of shavings on the floor were among the most vivid recurring memories

and helped to confirm his direction toward architecture. Another experience with his grandmother stimulated his lifelong "obsession" with fish. Every Thursday through much of his childhood, he would later recall, "We'd go to the Jewish market, we'd buy a live carp, we'd take it home . . . we'd put it in the bathtub and I would play with this . . . fish for a day . . . until she killed it and made gefilte fish."

Frank also learned many of his grandparents' cultural values from his mother, Thelma, who passed them on, reinforced, to her children. She had studied music at the Hamburg Institute, a Toronto conservatory, and had been involved with the local Yiddish theater. This was only a substitute, however, for the law career she had wanted. Forbidden by her traditional father from pursuing such an "inappropriate" course, she would later study law at the ripe age of sixty. Yet if Thelma's parents disapproved of her proposed legal career, they took an even dimmer view of her choice of a husband.

From the Caplans' middle-class perspective, Irving Goldberg was from the wrong side of the tracks. His parents had also emigrated from Poland, but had fared less well in New York than the Caplans had in Toronto. Irving was born in Brooklyn in 1900, though brighter prospects in Toronto led the Goldbergs to Canada when he was an infant. There they developed a family business called Tip Top Tailors, the promise of which was cut prematurely short by the senior Goldberg's accidental death by mercury poisoning in 1911. The widow and children returned to New York, this time to the poor Lower East Side of Manhattan, where Irving, age eleven, became a Hell's Kitchen street urchin. The familiar outlet for this tough "dead-end kid" was boxing and wrestling that evolved from street fighting to Golden Gloves respectability. The seamy attractions of the fight world would pass from Irving to Frank who would continue through mid-life to work out as a boxer and earn, as well, a belt in full-contact karate.

Like his father before him, Irving also drifted north from New York to Toronto, where he worked in various small business enterprises and where, even more significantly, he met and married Thelma Caplan. Like her father, Sam, he at one time had a hardware store; at another point he ran a grocery store. In the latter capacity, he won an award at the Canadian National Exhibition for store-window dressing, a collage of foods in the form of an American flag. "It was proto Jasper Johns," his son later observed. Irving's innate aesthetic sense was also expressed in a moderate drawing ability which he enjoyed indulging with Frank and his sister Doreen. As an elementary school teacher, Doreen would later develop the family penchant for design into a noted program of classroom "city-building."

After hardware and groceries, Irving developed a business that sold pinball and slot machines and various electronic recreational media. Frank would remember accompanying him to carnivals, where he called upon customers, and to Chicago, where he bought the

machines. While Frank was in grade school, Irving moved his business and his family to Timmins, Ontario, north of Toronto. It was a relatively prosperous and happy time. Thelma was active in such Jewish women's organizations as Hadassah, in which she invariably made her way to the top as president. Frank was a good student, particularly in math. He sold newspapers, belonged to the Boy Scouts, and began to discover girls, but such pleasures were darkened by the increasing degree of anti-Semitism he began to experience as he entered his teens. He was given the ironic nickname of "Fish" by his tormentors, presumably to suggest bad odor, and he would not realize until much later that "fish" was a Christian symbol. His ambivalent identity with the image, however, would last until exorcised in his fish sculptures of the 1980s.

The painful discrimination evoked by his Jewishness estranged him from the religious commitments that his mother and his grandparents had. Far from representing orthodox rigidity, his parents' generation even celebrated Christmas. Still, the ritual Bar Mitzvah seemed to Frank to be a "farce" and he soon teamed up with a high school classmate to write a treatise in defense of atheism.

In the mid-1940s, the family suffered an economic blow as slot machines were declared illegal in Canada and Irving lost his business. Shortly after the end of the war, they moved back to Toronto where he struggled with a small enterprise that produced wooden trays with decals on them. His declining health, following a heart attack, convinced them that he needed a more hospitable climate. One brother and a cousin already lived in Los Angeles. Another brother was moving there from Detroit. So, in 1947, like countless other seekers of health and fortune before them, the Goldbergs moved to southern California.

For fifty dollars a month they rented a small apartment at 9th and Burlington in downtown Los Angeles, a few blocks from the site of the Loyola Law School where thirty-five years later Frank would design a virtually new campus. Though Irving was ill, he had to work, first as a truck driver, then in a liquor store. Being truly poor for the first time in her life unnerved his wife. Clearly they could no longer afford to support their son, but if he could get a job, he could live at home. For the time being, college was out of the question. Meanwhile, Irving's more prosperous brothers furnished their teenage nephew with welcome diversions from the grim realities.

As a popular bartender at "Barney's Beanery," Uncle Willy had, over the years, acquired an impressive list of Hollywood contacts. Frank would later recall that meeting such movie stars as Robert Mitchum and Ida Lupino was equivalent to a visit to another planet. An even starker contrast to Frank's acquaintances in the neighborhood of 9th and Burlington was Uncle Willy's incongruous friendship with the suave actor, George Sanders. As part of the young man's initiation to Los Angeles, the two arranged for the innocent teenager a lurid encounter at the splashy Hotel Yucca with a bona fide French prostitute.

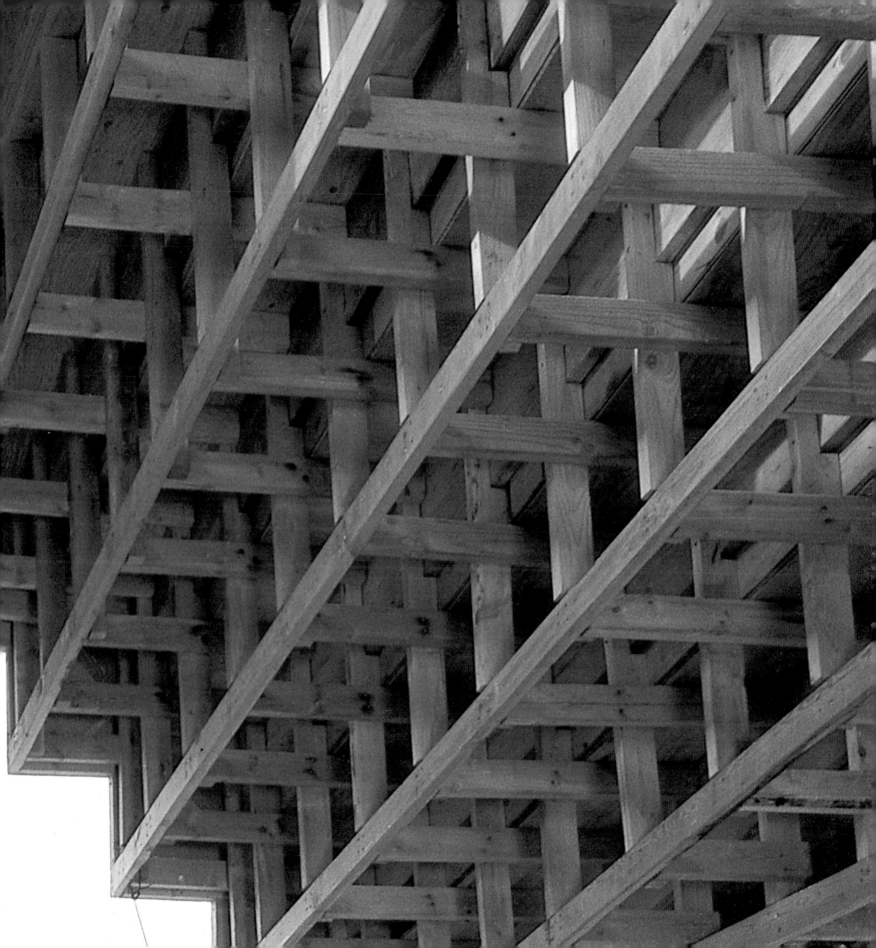

Uncle Harry, a barber, and his wife, Beulah, had changed their surname from Goldberg to Gaylord and had given their son the impressive name of Hartley. Aunt Beulah, Frank remembered, was a warm and fabulous person, a quintessential "Hollywood" character, who had conducted her own all-woman orchestra. From another cousin, a manufacturer of breakfast nooks, Frank got a job as a truck driver, delivering and installing the nooks throughout the region. Most of the customers were ordinary Angelinos but the list also included Hollywood celebrities. Frank's favorite discoveries among the latter were Roy Rogers and Dale Evans, who took him into their "home and hearts," included him in their annual Christmas caroling, and casually introduced him to their friend Bob Hope.

Other less famous clients included the parents of Anita Snyder, with whom Frank would fall in love and ultimately marry in 1952. Anita's father was a pharmacist in San Fernando Valley who did not approve of higher education for women, even for his intelligent daughter. Hence, Anita, after graduating from high school, took a business course and became a legal secretary. As with many couples in the postwar 1950s, her job made it possible for her husband to go to college. "When I met Anita," Frank confessed, "I was a duck out of water. She helped me to get grounded."

While driving the truck and delivering breakfast nooks, Frank had taken night courses at Los Angeles City College, but when he got a whiff of the better life at the University of Southern California from his cousin Hartley Gaylord, who was a student there, he drifted to U.S.C. First as a part-time and summer school student, then as a regularly matriculating undergraduate, his first mentor was Glen Lukens, a professor of ceramics. Recognizing his student's potential design talents, Lukens recommended that he consider studying architecture and introduced him to his friend, the architect Raphael Soriano. Frank was subsequently admitted to the U.S.C. School of Architecture, where he became friendly with Arnold Schreier, a graduate student in the school. Through Schreier, he met the photographer Julius Shulman and other leading figures in the city's architectural circles. With Schreier, he also designed an addition to a house in the Hollywood Hills, his first constructed work. The two spent their weekends looking at architecture from the older monuments of Wright, Schindler, and Neutra to the more recent work of Harwell Harris, Quincy Jones and the *Arts + Architecture* Case Study Program. It was a period of ferment in Los Angeles architecture.

The most influential faculty members at U.S.C. at the time included Calvin Straub, Si Eisner, Garrett Eckbo, Edgardo Contini and Gregory Ain, who was particularly memorable for his sophisticated ability to relate architecture to culture. Few other architects, Frank would recall, could so convincingly quote James Joyce to make an architectural point. A fellow student, Gregory Walsh, had similar gifts, especially in his passionate knowledge of music. A pianist who would subsequently make professional recordings, Walsh was also an ardent student of history and had an ability to express himself in writing that Frank admittedly lacked and envied. The two became friends and enjoyed working together. Their graphic styles were so similar, in fact, that the two could draw on the same sheet of paper and later be unable to distinguish one's work from the other. When each became bored with his own thesis project, they simply exchanged and finished each other's. Later, as Gehry's most constant associate, Walsh would develop a patience for detail that Frank himself found impossibly tedious. Yet Walsh would insist that, throughout the years, Gehry prevailed as the creative catalyst and provided the essential professional leadership.

In addition to formal school projects at U.S.C., Frank also drew illustrations for art professor Keith Crown's *Cross-Cultural Magazine.* One memorable composition was a series of views of the school mascot Tommy Trojan, bearing Christian, Jewish and Islamic insignia. During his last years in architecture school, Frank worked part time for Victor Gruen Associates, where he gained valuable experience and made important contacts, most notably with Gruen, himself, who greatly influenced his views on city planning. Upon graduation from U.S.C. in 1954 he began to work full time for Gruen before being drafted into the U.S. Army.

It was also at this time that he and Anita decided to change their surname. But the new name would make no sense if the whole family did not accept it. His mother and sister agreed to it. His father understandably showed greater reluctance since the name had long been his and his ancestors. "I think he was hurt by it," Frank later observed. Estranged from certain aspects of Judaism since adolescence, the new guilt incurred by denying his heritage forced Gehry ironically to think more about it. Gradually over the years it had the palpable effect of making him search more intensely for the roots the name change had partially severed and to appreciate more fully the importance of his Jewishness.

In 1955, with Anita, a young daughter, and another on the way, Private first class Gehry arrived at Fort Benning, Georgia. He was quickly rescued from a tedious clerk-typist job by a general who discovered his architectural background and put him to work designing enlisted men's dayrooms. With what seemed to be a virtually unlimited budget, Gehry worked out many of his "Wrightian fantasies" particularly in his furniture designs. Some of the pieces were so popular, he recalled, that they were transferred surreptitiously to the officers' club. The Fort Benning landscapes of "temporary" structures of corrugated metal, plywood and asphalt shingles were to reappear subliminally in a new incarnation in Gehry's work of the 1970s.

The interest in urban planning engendered at U.S.C. and his contact with Victor Gruen persuaded Gehry that he should study planning on

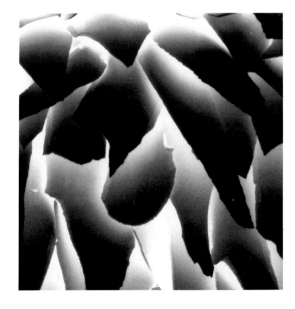

the graduate level. With the help of his former professors, Eisner and Eckbo, he was admitted in the fall of 1956 to the Harvard Graduate School of Design, but he quickly discovered that "planning" at Harvard was too abstract for his tastes and was grounded too heavily in the statistical social sciences. He, therefore, abandoned the idea of a degree in planning and became a special student, auditing lectures throughout the university. He was particularly impressed by Arthur Schlesinger, Jr., John Kenneth Galbraith and Pitirim Sorokin. The intellectual riches at Harvard stimulated Gehry's penchant for reading and his lifelong pursuit of new ideas. He took courses with Joseph Hudnut and particularly enjoyed the philosophical walking tours with him through the old Boston neighborhoods. Through him, Gehry discovered the European modernists, particularly Le Corbusier. Yet he also shared Hudnut's enthusiasm for the rich historic architecture of America and Europe and slowly began to realize that the Dean was actually struggling against the grip of the Bauhaus and its anti-historical influence on architectural education and design.

During his year at Harvard, Gehry worked part time in the Boston offices of Hideo Sasaki and Perry, Shaw, Hepburn and Dean. In 1957 he returned to Los Angeles for a brief stint with Pereira and Luckman before resuming his old position with Victor Gruen, where he worked until 1960. There he handled increasingly large jobs and was consequently disappointed to be continually passed over for promotion. This convinced him that he should leave Gruen and that he needed to get away from Los Angeles as well.

The discovery through Hudnut of architectural history had persuaded him that he should live for a while in Europe, and in 1961 he and Anita and their two young daughters moved to Paris, where he worked for over a year in the office of André Rémondet. Well served by his French-speaking Canadian education, he thrived as he explored the architecture of Europe. He made pilgrimages to Le Corbusier's chapel at Ronchamp and his monastery at La Tourette and to the German baroque treasures of Balthasar Neumann. Most of all, he was drawn to the Romanesque buildings of France and Germany, particularly Worms Cathedral, and he felt angry that his modernist mentors at U.S.C. had failed to introduce him to these architectural miracles.

Though he would largely continue for the next decade to design within the prevailing modernist canon, he would slowly begin in the 1970s to explore more consciously the expressive possibilities of historical references and the relationship of architecture to painting and sculpture. Though from time to time he might slip into such clichés as the lamentation over the "burden of culture," he would in such works as the Loyola Law School demonstrate that the legacies of "culture" and "history" need not be burdensome after all.

In 1962, Gehry returned from Europe to set up his own practice in Los Angeles.

The rest—as the saying goes—is "history."

Throughout the 1960s, 1970s and 1980s, the vicissitudes of life continued to shape and reflect the changing contours of Gehry's work. By 1966, a "conflict of egos" led to the breakup of his first marriage. Ten years later, after a renascent bachelorhood, he married a Panamanian émigré, Berta Isabel Aguilera, a woman of beauty, intelligence and quiet independence, whose critical sympathy for his work and his mission never compromised her own sense of identity. The two young sons of his ripe middle age complemented his pleasure in the daughters he fathered in the 1950s.

Of almost equal importance in these years of personal and artistic ferment was his friend, the psychologist, Milton Wexler, many of whose patients were painters, sculptors, writers, actors and other creative artists. "I first went to Milton," Gehry recalled, "because my world wasn't functioning very well. He was the first shrink to engage me intellectually." Through Wexler, Gehry got to know more artists who in turn introduced him to their own friends and patrons. Through the 1970s and 1980s, he became conscious of the impact, both personally and professionally, not only of Louis Danziger and Ron Davis, who became important clients, but of such artists as Ed Moses, Larry Bell, Robert Irwin, Jasper Johns, Robert Rauschenberg, Ellsworth Kelly, Carl Andre, Michael Heizer, Billy Al Bengston, Ed Ruscha, Richard Serra, Claes Oldenburg and Andy Warhol. The actors Ben Gazzara and Janice Rule and the playwright Lillian Hellman also became stimulating and influential friends. Their way of making art strongly affected his way of making architecture. In Gehry's own art, Philip Johnson became his most supportive mentor. Yet, by the 1970s, Gehry himself had become a mentor to countless young architects who passed through his office or were influenced by his work.

When he first approached Wexler, he had wondered if the "treatment" might indeed solve personal problems but render him less fertile artistically. Wexler convinced him that therapy would make him a stronger architect. And ultimately, Gehry was certain, that turned out to be the case.

Slowly he learned to sublimate the anger, pain and fear of existing in a crazy, hostile world to architectural statements *about* those tensions. Frequently via irony and a sometimes dark humor, there crept into his work elements of light and hope. Reflecting his favored aesthetic of "buildings under construction," his work would frequently suggest "unfinished business" or the poignant incompleteness of all human existence. It would also, paradoxically, suggest *arrested* decadence in a world continually dying and being born. His buildings of the late 1970s, with studs tossed and "frozen" just before the "explosion,"

O'Neill Hay Barn   1968
San Juan Capistrano, California

The barn was functionally so simple that it was enticing to deal with it as a sculptural object. The things to be solved were minimal. You just had to keep the rain off the hay: the hay was stacked high at one end; the farm vehicles were at the other end, much lower, so I tilted the roof. I chose telephone poles for the framework, because it was the least expensive way to get a rigid frame that would allow the roof to be structurally uncomplicated. I liked the way the light hit corrugated metal and the tilted piece of metal reflecting the sky could, I thought, absolutely blend into the sky so that you wouldn't see the plane, so it would become one with the sky. That did happen a couple of times when I was there.

could be read as a metaphor of the end of the world or could be seen conversely as disaster averted, with things pulled back to safety "just in time."

Critics of the 1970s and 1980s would enjoy labeling Gehry a "rule breaker," yet, if he was breaking the rules, they were rules of a different order from his own. He obeyed his own rules, the rules he had forged over a lifetime of experience. "Why should we honor those who die upon the field of battle," William Butler Yeats had asked. " . . . a man may show as reckless a courage in entering into the abyss of himself."

Gehry's own tastes in poetry are occasionally more sentimental, though no less revealing, as in "The Great Lover" by the Englishman Rupert Brooke. In its laundry list of favored things, tough and fragile, ordinary and arcane, Gehry recognizes lifelong references as well as continuing needs and preferences. "These I have loved:" Brooke asserts as preamble:

Wet roofs, beneath the lamp-light;
. . . the blue bitter smoke of wood; . . .
And flowers themselves, that sway through sunny hours,
Dreaming of moths that drink them under the moon;
Then, the cool kindliness of sheets, that soon
Smooth away trouble; and the rough male kiss
Of blankets; grainy wood; . . .
Unpassioned beauty of a great machine;
The benison of hot water; furs to touch; . . .
Hair's fragrance, and the musty reek that lingers
About dead leaves . . .

Holes in the ground; and voices that do sing;
Voices in laughter, too; and body's pain, . . .
Firm sands; the little dulling edge of foam
That browns and dwindles as the wave goes home;
And washen stones, gay for an hour; the cold
Graveness of iron; . . .
All these have been my loves. . . .

But the best I've known
Stays here, and changes, breaks, grows old . . .

———————————

The child has been, as always, the father of the man.

I think the design of the barn had to do with my beginning interest in very cheap materials growing out of my Victor Gruen experiences. Working with developers, seeing them always trying to make things cheaper, I was intrigued with the idea of making something inexpensive and getting more out of it. The materials didn't matter; what mattered was the concept and the feeling of the building that could be made with inexpensive materials.

Concord Pavilion   1975-1977
Concord, California

Section Looking South

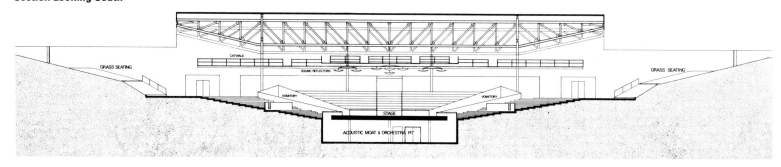

At the foot of Mt. Diablo, the pavilion was placed in a natural bowl among Concord's rolling hills. Its square roof spans a 400 square foot performance space. The acoustician Christopher Jaffe and Gehry worked closely to achieve the sound for which this facility is famous.

Section Looking East

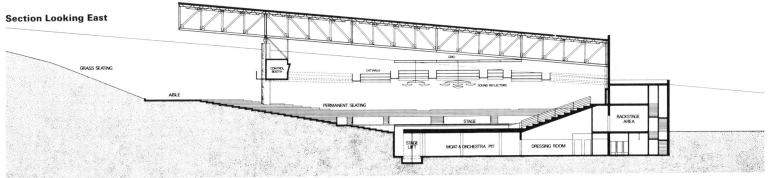

GRASS SEATING

AISLE

PERMANENT SEATING

CONTROL BOOTH

CATWALK

GRID

SOUND REFLECTORS

STAGE

STAGE LIFT

MOAT & ORCHESTRA PIT

DRESSING ROOM

BACKSTAGE AREA

Ron Davis Studio

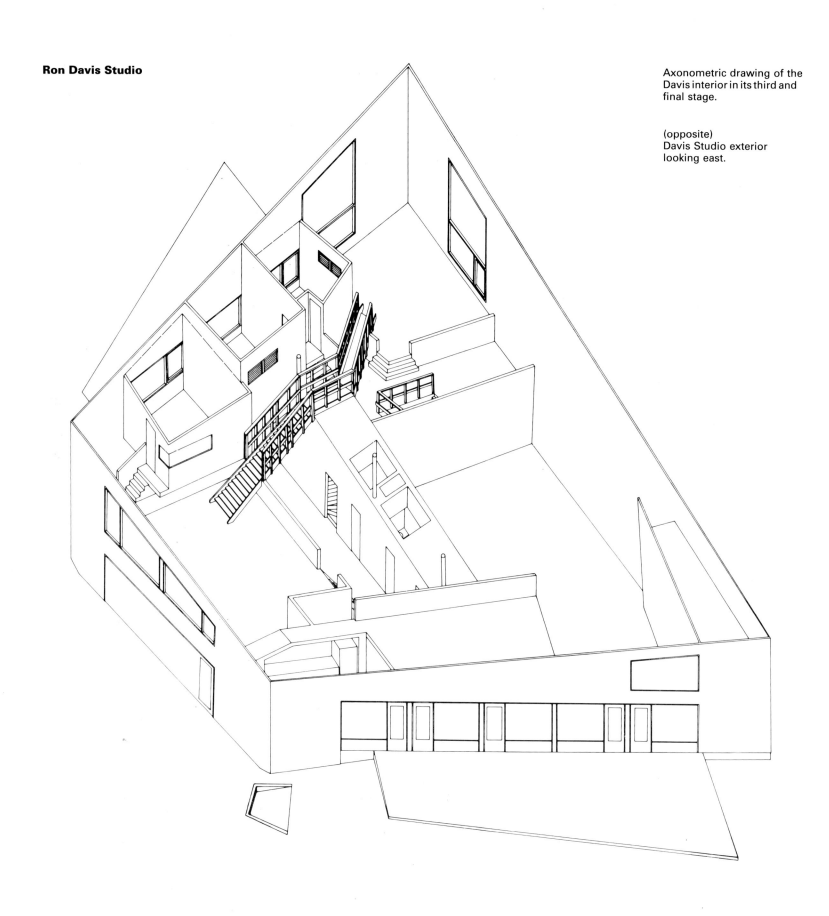

Axonometric drawing of the
Davis interior in its third and
final stage.

(opposite)
Davis Studio exterior
looking east.

Rosemarie Haag Bletter

Frank Gehry's
Spatial Reconstructions

Frank Gehry's architecture cannot be readily categorized as either modern or postmodern. His work exists outside the strictures of ready-made labels. The unruly, wild appearance of many of his buildings goes against the grain of those who admire the carefully controlled structures more typical of architectural design. We might call him the Frank Furness of the twentieth century because of the robust articulation of his forms. Even though his works hardly look like historicizing nineteenth-century buildings, they have something in common with the Victorian worship of pre-Renaissance primitivism as well as the Victorians' elevation of architectural "character" over the gentler and more traditional "beauty" or "harmony." Gehry's comparative isolation in the contemporary architectural scene does not mean, however, that his works exist entirely outside any cultural context.

In Gehry's case the most immediate references are, to start with, the painting and sculpture of his California friends. As he said in 1976:

My approach to architecture is different. I search out the work of artists, and use art as a means of inspiration. I try to rid myself and the other members of the firm, of the burden of culture and look for new ways to approach the work. I want to be open-ended. There are no rules, no right or wrong. I'm confused as to what's ugly and what's pretty.[1]

He surely does not share Frank Lloyd Wright's aversion to the art of his contemporaries. On the contrary, Gehry's own house is filled with art. For almost two years the artist Chuck Arnoldi, whose work Gehry owns, had his studio adjacent to Gehry's office in the same small building in Venice (an interior door, usually kept unlocked, connected the two work spaces). Ron Davis, another artist friend (a major work of his was long on display in Gehry's house), became an important early client. Gehry (like the architect Peter Eisenman, who claims to be working outside cultural reference points) may not be able to free

1. Janet Nairn, "Frank Gehry: The Search for a 'No Rules' Architecture," *Architectural Record,* June 1976, p 95.

Ron Davis Studio   1970-1972
Malibu, California

Ron Davis came to me after he had seen the O'Neill Hay Barn. He wanted to build a studio and residence in Malibu. The ideas for the house grew out of perspective, which Ron and I were both interested in. It also dealt with the way artists live in large studio spaces, making their own space within that. I thought we could make a single large shell for each of the buildings—one for the residence and one for the studio—and that the shell could be sculpturally strong and still maintain a kind of flexibility inside. The other issue was to try to place the buildings in a relationship that would take advantage of every inch of the site. I wanted the building itself to be sculpturally related to the earth that it's sitting on and to control the space around it. This house, which finally was the only building built, became a studio as well.

himself completely from the "burden of culture." But when Gehry alludes to artistic referents, he aligns himself with an evolving cultural context that is teetering on the edge. Further, the artistic milieu from which his ideas spring is less tied to tradition and norms than architecture. Architecture, because of its usual teamwork between client and contractor and because of its tremendous costs, responds to cultural shifts somewhat more sluggishly than painting.

With his design for the Malibu, California studio and residence for Ron Davis (1970-1972) Gehry initiated his own startling commentary on the convoluted relationship between art and architecture. A trapezoidal plan and elevations create a subtly enigmatic form, referring to but also exaggerating our normal perspectival perception of orthogonal architecture. In conventional buildings with right angles we know that a rectangle is *seen* as a trapezoid. Through our early experience of deciphering the true proportion of objects in space, we deduce from the visual evidence that a shape read as a trapezoid is usually a rectangle. Although our man-made world is full of rectangular forms, unless we occupy an ideal vantage point centered directly in front or above (hard to achieve with buildings), we almost never perceive such shapes in their Platonic states, with right angles intact. What we do see is nearly always a slightly foreshortened figure, i.e. a trapezoid. Both our visual perception of a trapezoid and our conceptual deduction of a rectangle are, of course, elements of reality. But toying with a conflation of the world of perception and conception provides a fascinating game for Gehry's tricky sensibility. In the Ron Davis Studio any automatic deduction from perceived to built reality is confounded by his construction of what is usually only a perceptual reality, i.e., trapezoidal forms. It is as if a Renaissance architect had tried to use perspective in the execution, not just the rendering, of a building.

The Ron Davis Studio is more than a restatement of perspectival representation, however. It also engages us in a dialogue with the oeuvre of Davis. Davis's most characteristic works at the time his studio was executed were thin, two-dimensional wall pieces that give the illusion of spatial perspective. An apparent image of folded bands is created through a series of attached trapezoidal forms that can be associated with diminution in space. To be sure, the illusion of depth perception rendered in two dimensions is a venerable tradition in the history of art. But whereas point perspective was commonly used in pre-modern painting to evoke a specific time-space setting for narrative subject matter, Davis's allusion to perspective is within an entirely abstracted, geometric context. His reference to perspective functions much like the figures of optical illusions: because of the absence of naturalistic reference points, the geometric images can be read alternately as flat trapezoids or as rectangles rendered perspectivally.

Gehry has taken Davis's system of two-dimensional optical illusions a step further into spatial artifice by imposing forced perspective on a

Interior views of the Davis Studio demonstrate the integration of the artist's professional and domestic activities.

fully three-dimensional object. This approach differs radically from the forced perspective of stage design, which creates an illusion of *naturalistic* space. The Davis Studio, although a simple shed, achieves a high degree of visual complexity because of Gehry's manipulation of our perceptual expectations. The resulting spatial ambiguity is not sculptural in the normal sense of that term. It cannot be compared with the full-bodied—almost expressionist—muscular forms of, for instance, Le Corbusier's chapel at Ronchamp. The spatial effects in the Davis Studio are created by means of flat planes and distorted pictorial elements. Superimposing a perceptual operation onto a physical object, Gehry has undermined both systems of knowledge, the perceptual and the physical, into an illuminating and ultimately anti-rational experience. He has re-created a quasi-space out of abstracted spatial two-dimensional illusions. The distorted enclosures in Gehry's work, inspired by a perceptually elusive art, have little in common with the flatness of ordinary walls.

The studio's design is by no means a simple response to Davis's paintings. A friend of Davis long before he received the commission for this building, Gehry has said that he taught Davis the use of point perspective with which he was apparently not familiar. The very presence of a geometric illusionism in Davis's work is therefore, according to this account, partly due to Gehry's influence on Davis at an earlier stage. In designing the studio, Gehry wanted to "build a shape that would be understandable to Davis." But Davis is said to have been initially intimidated by the new space. For about two years after he moved into his new work space, he stopped painting altogether and only gradually returned to doing small drawings and eventually, as he learned to take up the challenge of the building, did he come back to large-scale works.[2] Distorted perspectives recur in many of Gehry's later buildings, notably in the interior office space of the Mid-Atlantic Toyota Offices, Glen Burnie, Maryland (1978), where space dividers and suspended panels of chain-link fencing create a lyrical interior landscape of rising and descending forms vaguely reminiscent of Japanese landscapes.[3] Though not in the least representational, this uncommon office space brings to mind the irregularity of nature.

Gehry's response to the art and sculpture of his time, and, more specifically, his transfer of illusionistic geometries back to a full spatial presence, contain a superficial resemblance to Le Corbusier's architecture of the 1920s in which the shallowly layered effects of Cubism are reinterpreted as architectural space.[4] But despite Gehry's similar method of creating an ambiguous architecture inspired by an abstracted space in painting, his work does not share the equally characteristic dematerialized effect of Le Corbusier's white villas. Gehry's architecture, by contrast, has an overwhelming material palpability. In Gehry's work the strong presence of, say, metal or plywood, is constantly at odds with the spatial dissonance with which these same materials were

2. Interview with Frank Gehry, 29 November 1985. But also see Susan C. Larsen, "Imagine a Space, a Form a World: The Paintings of Ron Davis," *Art News,* January 1980, p 105.
3. Martin Filler, "Perfectly Frank—Mid-Atlantic Toyota Distributors Warehouse and Offices, Glen Burnie, Md.," *Progressive Architecture,* July 1979, pp 62-65.
4. Colin Rowe and Robert Slutzky, "Transparency: Literal and Phenomenal," *The Mathematics of the Ideal Villa and Other Essays* (Cambridge, MA: MIT Press, 1976), pp 160-183. First published in *Perspecta 8,* 1963, and *Perspecta 13/14,* 1971. See review, Rosemarie Haag Bletter, "Opaque Transparency," *Oppositions,* 13, Summer 1978, pp 121-126.

assembled. His nonobjective composition coupled with the assertiveness of the materials is more readily comparable to the Abstract Expressionists' startling combinations of non-representational forms with a simultaneous emphasis on the tactile qualities of paint and brushstroke.

In its architectural imagery, Gehry's work is closest in spirit to Russian Constructivism. In architectural design, Constructivism grew out of contemporary debates in painting and sculpture. Through the example of Kasimir Malevich, a mystical, abstract strain began to suffuse the Cubo-Futurism of Russian artists. The Revolution of 1917, on the other hand, affected the polemics of the same group in an apparently contrary way: in an attempt to include references to the nature of ordinary work—and to avoid the esoteric aesthetics of high art—materials were often used as primitive, raw artifacts, a forceful crafting that seems intentionally undigested. Vladimir Tatlin's *Monument to the Third International* (1919-1920), Alexander Rodchenko's designs for kiosks (1919-1920), or Konstantin Melnikov's Soviet Pavilion for the International Exhibition of Decorative Arts in Paris (1925) all reflect this contradictory inclusion of formal abstraction together with the workaday look of the materials. Gehry's architecture in its cryptic overall design and its simultaneous tough, robust display of lowly materials is in this respect akin to Constructivist design, if not to its full political polemics. It is true that Le Corbusier, as early as the 1930s, occasionally worked with the primitive effects of rubble walls. These, however, are echoes of local vernacular traditions and in his pre-World War II work rarely take over the whole structure. By the time he turned to a broader primitivism after the war—later called New Brutalism—his experiment with Cubist layered space was over. In Corbusier's work, therefore, we do not get the unusual conjunction of abstracted space with an almost nineteenth-century display of the nature of materials. Beyond a similar interest in the evocation of a painterly space and in a self-conscious primitivism, Gehry does not respond directly to the designs of Le Corbusier or even Vladimir Tatlin, but to a Modernism as practiced in California in the second half of the twentieth century.

Another jolting juxtaposition in Gehry's design method is his exceptional combination of truly ordinary building materials, corrugated metal and plywood. This seemingly unnatural union produces a collision between the industrial, high-tech associations of corrugated metal and the low-tech nature of plywood, most familiar in temporary structures or homemade carpentry. Like some great protective shield, the harsh corrugated metal covers the exterior of the Davis Studio. The interior, by contrast, has the warmer and rougher tonalities of wooden panels and exposed beams. The antithesis between the factorylike exterior and the rambling, informal interior with its lofts and wooden staircases could not be more extreme. Both qualities, the high-tech and low-tech, are expressions of an American—and particularly

Cabrillo Marine Museum   1979
San Pedro, California

In an original scheme by another architect the
Cabrillo Museum was designed to be in a
parklike setting. That failed to get approval in
the community, and circumstances changed.
They then selected a parking lot as the place
to build. That asphalt site with the city, the
boats and the hardware of shipping had a
chain link fence around it. All those things

were contextual—they set the context.
    There was an army base on one side of the
site, the ocean on the other side, and lots of
parking and boat storage in between. I chose
to play with that context and decided,
because of the budget, to make the buildings
very simple boxes, and to develop a courtyard
with the administration building as an object

Looking toward the Pacific
from the hill behind the
Cabrillo Museum.

**sitting in it. All of this is connected with an
ephemeral gauze of chain link, used in a
sculptural way. Those forms play against the
sky and against the environment that I chose
to complement and become involved with.**

Californian—mentality wherein pride in advanced technology coexists uneasily with the indomitable reliance on a do-it-yourself approach. In the California architecture of the earlier twentieth century we were not likely to encounter the industrial and arts-and-crafts tradition so overtly in one and the same building, however. For example, while Charles and Henry Greene's Gamble House in Pasadena (1908-1909) is practically a handmade object, Richard Neutra's Von Sternberg House in Northridge, California (1935), gives the appearance of an efficient machine. On the other hand, Gehry contraposes a harsh with a homey expression in a single structure.

The unexpected and confrontational application of run-of-the-mill materials to non-commercial building types becomes characteristic of most of Gehry's later buildings. The best known among his mature works is his most idiosyncratic design, his own house in Santa Monica (1977-1978). Indeed, because he was his own client, a high degree of experimentation was possible. For this reason, though it is a fairly small project, it signals more clearly than many of his other works his full range of intentions.

Here, in addition to corrugated metal, chain-link fencing is used to define exterior areas, if not to enclose space. Like corrugated metal, chain-link fencing is normally seen in the context of industrial plants or nondescript residential backyards. Even more than corrugated metal, the fencing material, because it does not provide for architectural enclosure, seems subversive. In his Santa Monica house Gehry used it to create a series of transparent screens in and around his building. Its presumed ugliness is transformed into gossamer webs. He has used chain-link fencing more extensively since then in the Cabrillo Marine Museum, San Pedro, California (1979) and in the Santa Monica Place shopping mall, Santa Monica (1973-1980). In some of his environmental sculptures the artist Robert Irwin has recently turned to plastic-coated, colored chain link as a space-defining material, as in his *9 Spaces, 9 Trees* for the Public Safety Building Plaza, Seattle (1980-1983) and in *Two Running Violet V Forms* for the University of California, San Diego (1981-1983). Gehry had proposed chain-link fencing for an unexecuted walk-through sculpture for Long Beach Park as early as 1976.[5] According to Gehry, Irwin, a longtime friend, visited his office specifically to study the use of chain link after seeing Santa Monica Place. Gehry adds, however, that he had been influenced in the first place by Irwin's scrim pieces. Although organized differently than Irwin's scrim, for Gehry "chain link has the attributes of fabric."[6] Through such high-art applications we may in the long run learn to change our association of chain-link fencing with semi-industrial ugliness in the same way that Le Corbusier forced us to rethink our reaction to concrete.

To Gehry's neighbors, however, his house seems like an alien intrusion amidst its setting of unpretentious bungalows. Gehry has complained:

There's a smugness about middle-class neighborhoods that bothered me, I guess. Everybody has their camper truck in front, everybody has their boat in front. There's a lot of activity related to hardware and junk, and cars and boats . . . And the neighbors have come around and told me . . . 'I don't like your house.' And I say: 'What about your boat in the backyard? What about your camper truck? It's the same material, it's the same aesthetic.' They say: 'Oh, no, no, that's normal.' I'm always surprised that other people don't see it . . . it just seems so obvious to me, that one should use chain link, because it's such a pervasive material.[7]

To those of his neighbors who are unable to form new visual associations, it will remain a provocative eyesore. Like an unwelcome intruder, it even has been the object of a sniper's bullet. Gehry introduces a note of caution about the dramatic possibilities of this event, however. A local police officer told him that other houses in the neighborhood have been hit as well. For this reason Gehry believes that the shot in the dark cannot be interpreted as architectural criticism.[8]

Despite its disquieting exterior, Gehry's Santa Monica house was only a renovation of an existing building. After buying a rather unexceptional California bungalow of around 1920, the architect proceeded to deconstruct part of the old building and to surround it with a new envelope. The shell of the pink-walled original house remains partly visible from the outside through the transparent elements of the new structure. As Gehry has explained it:

My wife, Berta, found this beautiful . . . anonymous little house, and I decided to remodel it, and . . . since it was my own building . . . explore ideas I'd had about the materials I used here: corrugated metal and plywood, chain link . . . And, I was interested in making the old house appear intact inside the new house, so that, from the outside, you would be aware always that the old house was still there. You would feel like this old house was still there, and some guy just wrapped it in new materials, and you could see, as you looked through the windows—during the day or at night—you would see this old house sitting in there. And my intention was that the combination of both would make the old house richer and the new house would be richer by association with the old . . .[9]

On the exterior of the Santa Monica house, corrugated metal sheets are pierced at the corner and along the center of the north elevation by tilted, glazed cubic forms that function as windows for the dining area and kitchen. It looks as if crystalline formations are pushing outward through an armored shell. Higher up, at the attic level, above the entrance, chain-link screens reveal the roof of the old building nestling inside its new housing. Gehry's design generates his intended double image: a palimpsest of the house's history in which the viewer can read the old house quite literally through the forms of the new one. This is a modernist conception of historicizing possibilities devoid of

5. See *Architectural Record, op. cit.,* p 102.
6. Interview with Frank Gehry, 17 October 1985.
7. Transcript from documentary film *Beyond Utopia: Changing Attitudes in American Architecture,* interviews and narration by Rosemarie Haag Bletter and Martin Filler, Michael Blackwood Productions, 1983, pp 47-48.
8. Interview with Frank Gehry, 17 October 1985.
9. *Beyond Utopia, op. cit.,* p 46.

Gehry House

Initial sketch for the Gehry
House   1977
pencil on paper
8½ x 11
Collection Berta Gehry

Gehry House   1977-1978
Santa Monica, California

North facade of the Gehry House with its cubistic kitchen window and a view into the backyard through the tilted rectangle of an unglazed opening. Corrugated metal siding also surfaces the walls on the east side of the building.

My house. I'm afraid so much has been said about it that it is very difficult for me to add anything except that living there is very comfortable. It does leak a little and we're working on fixing that. The ideas in this house were continued into the Spiller House. They first saw the light of day, I guess, in the Familian House, and were actually built and tested in a house for Norton Simon on the beach in Malibu. The detailing in my house was the beginning, and in the next few projects we solved the technology, so they didn't leak as much. The predecessor for this, in concept, was the St. Ives House, in which we took an existing house and built a new house around it. In that case the new house was very much in the style of the old house, so it became a layered experience, but there wasn't a counterpoint. I think that led me to this next step. I probably wouldn't have taken this step had I not done the other.

the occasionally nostalgic eclecticism of the postmodernists.

Along one side, the wall of corrugated metal is extended beyond the confines of the house proper to form a screen wall between street and backyard. The interior of this metal wall is lined in plywood and it is supported from the inside with bracing beams as if to suggest the unstructured and makeshift feeling of this private play space. The same unpainted wooden textures are continued along the wall of the house that faces this secluded outdoor area. The metallic stolidity of the street facades thus yields to roughly finished wooden textures once we penetrate into the private realm of yard and house. To emphasize this point, inside the old section of the house Gehry has stripped most of the walls and ceilings down to their simple wooden framework. The exposed joists and laths form yet another historical layer in this dialogue between new and old structures. Gehry in fact has returned a portion of the old building to a temporary state that more than anything resembles its construction stage just before the final completion. This innermost decomposed core suggests, therefore, the pre-history of the original house. The "incomplete" core is enclosed by its intact, finished exterior, now partly internalized by the third layer, its contemporary mantle.

This view of the east facade reveals the pink wall of the original house.

I remember the early process of designing the house: I looked at the old house that my wife found for us to live in, and I thought it was kind of a dinky little cutesy-pie house. We had to do *something* to it. I couldn't live in it. That was Berta's intention.

Armed with very little money I decided to build a new house around the old house and try to maintain a tension between the two by having one define the other, and to have the feeling that the old house was intact within the new house, from the outside and from the

Gehry House

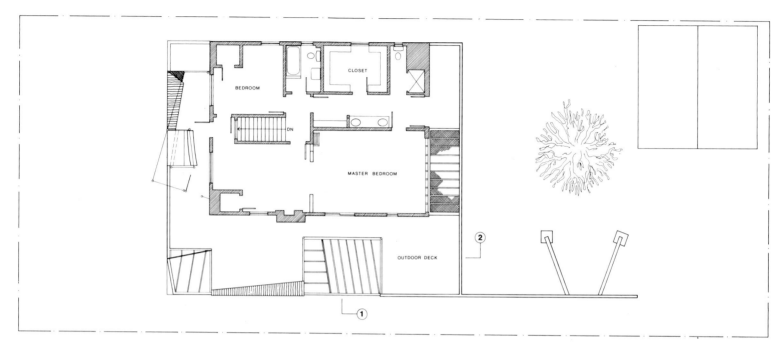

Second Floor Plan

N

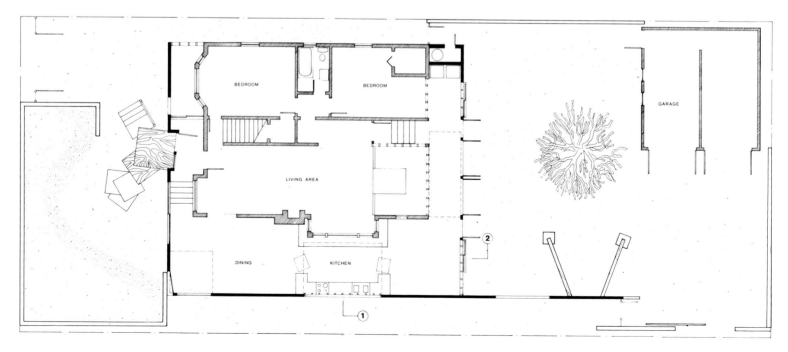

First Floor Plan

Bird's-eye view axonometric drawing of the Gehry House.

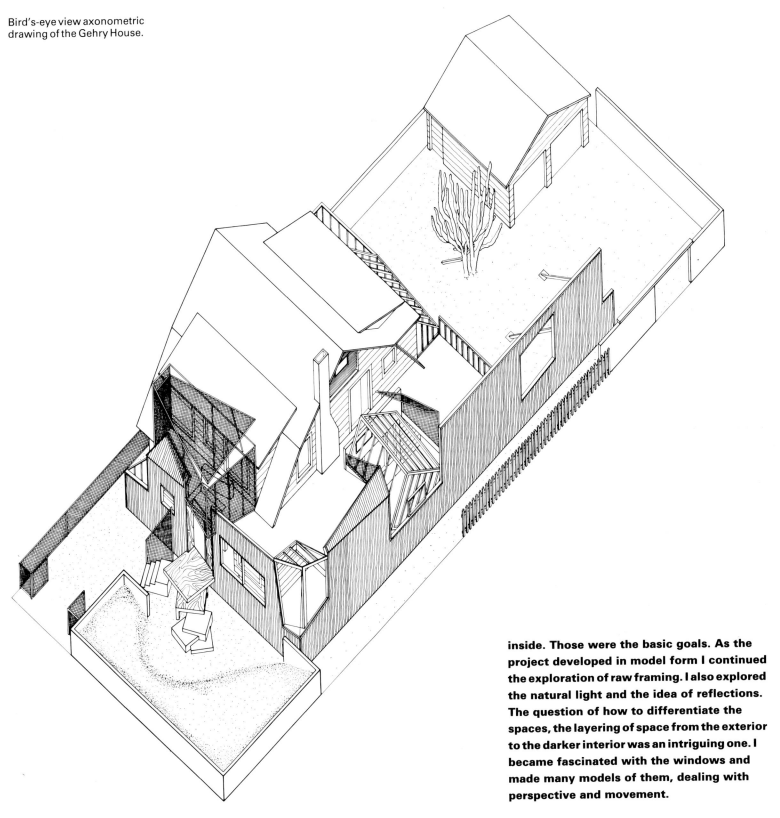

inside. Those were the basic goals. As the project developed in model form I continued the exploration of raw framing. I also explored the natural light and the idea of reflections. The question of how to differentiate the spaces, the layering of space from the exterior to the darker interior was an intriguing one. I became fascinated with the windows and made many models of them, dealing with perspective and movement.

Gehry House

Kitchen window on the north facade (left).

The second floor east balcony is enlivened by the patterns of chain-link fencing that surround it.

An informal dining area is located outside the north wall of the original house, in line with the new kitchen to its west.

The painted brick fireplace (right) is surrounded with raw plywood walls. Two armchairs, designed for the Berger, Berger law offices, Easy Edges tables and a footstool surround the fireplace. Edward Ruscha's print *Hollywood* hangs above the mantel.

A living room seating area is shown upholstered with industrial felt-covered foam rubber cushions (top, left) and in an earlier period with bare wood benches (below).

For instance, I was interested in the corner window, how you turn the corner. I thought of Duchamp's nude going down the staircase, and I tried to figure out how I could rotate the corner so as you walked around it, it would rotate. That's why that piece of glass slides beyond the corner. It works from the inside and outside to rotate the cube.

Gehry House

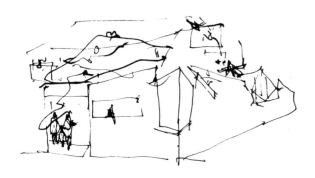

Early sketch of the Gehry
House northeast corner
window and front
entrance 1977
ink on paper
8⅛ x 10¾
Collection Fred Hoffman

The air of easygoing informality is enhanced by the unfinished look of Gehry's favored materials, corrugated metal, chain-link fencing and plywood. The heart and soul of the house are laid bare, so to speak, while the exterior is armored against a somewhat hostile neighborhood. In 1976 Gehry stressed the psychological fit of his architecture to the sensibilities of its inhabitants:

I design for minimal construction, by defining only the line or outer physical wall, and let the user define his own space and make it an intimate part of himself, so he will develop a relationship with the architecture . . . it is important to design a flexible space.[10]

He presumably was not talking about the flowing, open living rooms of Frank Lloyd Wright or Ludwig Mies van der Rohe, but rather about an emotional reciprocity between the interior and its occupants.

The sharp contrast between high-tech, glittery exterior and a casual, incomplete interior is even more acutely defined in the Santa Monica house than it had been in the Ron Davis Studio. This abrupt and disconnected definition of a separate inside and outside—so unlike the almost continuous indoor-outdoor spaces of modernists such as Ludwig Mies van der Rohe, Richard Neutra, Harwell Hamilton Harris, Gregory Ain or Pierre Koenig—may be a commentary on an American social condition that has become evident in architecture since the mid-1960s.

One can find the beginning of this phenomenon in Louis Kahn's two most influential works of that decade: his Richards Medical Research Building at the University of Pennsylvania, Philadelphia (1958-1961) and the Salk Institute of Biological Studies, La Jolla (1959-1965). There, facades and public spaces are not treated in a traditional manner. Barriers are thrown up between the buildings and their settings. No inviting, generous gestures toward the local context have been provided. The structures appear as thoroughly isolated incidents in their social environs. For instance, the perimeter of the Richards Medical Research Building is defined by towers inspired by those of San Gimignano. Although their function is not for defense against the enemy as at San Gimignano (Kahn's towers contain utilities and stairwells), the ring of towers that encircles the building nevertheless makes the visual impact of guard towers. Similarly, in Kahn's Salk Institute the main buildings hide behind a series of huge utility towers along the outer sides. They create a Great Wall of China effect, rather than a structure that reveals its function from a distance. The courtyard placed between the two parallel wings of the laboratories is thus more private than public in its general disposition. Kahn's institutional buildings, though visually powerful, turn their backs to the public. Space for social congregation is developed behind the safety of a defensive barrier.

To understand this radical shift in plan, one should compare it to public buildings of the early twentieth century in which grand stairways or U-shaped forecourts received the visitor with open arms. While the harshness of Kahn's forms may have been influenced by New Brutalism in Europe (Le Corbusier's late works have an existential monumentality), his specific arrangements vis-à-vis public space suggest more than noble alienation. They turn inward defensively. The increasing absence of social consensus, but especially the devastation of the public environment by the automobile in our laissez-faire society, may account for such a jarring introversion of built form in the United States.

In a sense, Kahn's buildings are symbolic of the contemporary nuclear society. Gehry has taken this kind of indirect architectural expression from the more public realm of Kahn's work to a residential setting, the private house. Where Frank Lloyd Wright's early prairie houses were superb evocations of the extended family as a social focus and anchor of the community at large, Gehry seems to define the breakup of the old pattern. The fragmentation of the family together with the intrusive presence of the car (which makes for a street full of strangers passing through) are the factors most responsible for the change. In her profile of Frank Gehry, Barbara Goldstein saw his reaction to impermanence and the car as a contextual, regional expression:

Southern California is full of images of building and rebuilding. From the ticky-tacky construction of its inner city commercial avenues to the massive housing tracts in Orange County, there are always new building and demolition going on. The area is also laced with industrial sites and military installations fenced off with chain link. Earthquakes, fires, and floods hardly instill a pervading feeling of permanence. Then there is the car. [11]

Gehry's use of present-day vernacular materials is indeed a specific local response, but their general configuration—a hard exterior protecting a cozy, internalized space—at the same time transcends any regionalism.

Gehry's larger public buildings are, like his houses, stylistically distinct from the works of Kahn. Where Kahn is overwhelmingly monumental, Gehry prefers to be low-key. Nevertheless, like Kahn, Gehry has chosen to internalize "public" space. Speaking about Gehry's Cabrillo Marine Museum, Goldstein writes:

Recently he has been 'exploding' his buildings, breaking them into several discrete volumes and tying these together with chain-link structures, arcades, or other purely visual devices. By working with the spaces in between buildings he is, in a sense, constructing a model of urban space inside his buildings. [12]

In another larger project, his more recent Loyola Law School in Los Angeles (1981-1984), situated in a drab area near downtown, the "urban" space is turned completely away from the street. The main facade appears fractured, rent asunder by a daring open stairway. Simple cylindrical drums are used to suggest colonnades. Gehry explains:

It's a minimal kind of postmodernism, if it is. But I would have done it anyway, because of the need to get . . . something that looked like courthouses and that looked like it had something to do with the

10. Janet Nairn, *op. cit.*
11. Barbara Goldstein, "Frank O. Gehry & Associates," *Progressive Architecture,* March 1980, p 71. This issue of *Progressive Architecture* contains several articles on Gehry's work.
12. Barbara Goldstein, "Spaces in Between: Cabrillo Marine Museum, Wilmington, Ca," *Ibid.,* p 78.

Gehry House

The kitchen, looking west. In this view, the exterior wall of the original house remains as a strong presence in the kitchen's south wall.

(opposite)
The raw wood framing of the dining room window (detail, top left) is echoed in the kitchen window, which

provides marvelous daylight for the tile-clad counter below.

The main kitchen window was the normal place to gash the metal on the outside, because it related to the main element of the old house, the bay window. I started a dialogue with that new kitchen window and the existing bay window, which is nice and geometric and very static and decorative. I became interested in opposing the bay window with a different kind of geometric activity, something that was more active. I

Partially stripped walls of the second floor master bed-sitting room reveal the original framework of the two-story house and achieve an "in-process" character similar to that admired by the architect in contemporary painting.

fantasized that when I closed in the box (the old house) there were ghosts in the house that would try to creep out, and this window was a cubist ghost. I became fascinated with that idea and started making models of windows that looked like the ghost of Cubism was trying to crawl out. It took about a month of work to figure out the window, and we used up all the money.

legal profession, the law school. I had just visited Rome as I was working on the design, and I got interested in the Roman Forum, with all the columns, broken, lying around, and I came back, and I had that kind of idea for this, but I think that having a few columns lying on the ground, might not have been too easily accepted. So that you have in effect, a stage set for a law school.[13]

This statement makes clear that in the late twentieth century it has become difficult to approach typological expression of a building with the confidence and grand design the Beaux-Arts generation of American architects was able to muster. Ironic gesture (the law school as stage set) serves therefore to disengage rather than involve the viewer, just as the school's public space is not truly urban in a traditional sense, but is self-contained. Furthermore, like Kahn in his late work, Gehry has become interested in the imagery of ruins. Although the conservative taste of his patrons for the Loyola Law School made the inclusion of fallen columns impossible, Gehry's intended device would have connoted impermanence within an institutional setting. While standing columns suggest a venerable Western history, in their fallen state their meaning would not have been so different from the chain-link fencing and plywood Gehry uses elsewhere. Ruins, the romantic, Piranesian metaphor for the passage of time, can readily be equated with contemporary images of impermanence.

Gehry's more recent tendency to "explode" buildings, to break them up into several discrete volumes, suggests on the surface a formalistic procedure. Gehry described his method as follows:

. . . it grows out of the House for a Filmmaker and my house and other houses I've been working on, which were sort of the testing ground for this breaking down of the parts into separate objects, having separate identities . . . almost a separate aesthetic. And using the richness of the parts to make a whole, which is like our cities are built. So, if you look at a city, that's what it is, only some of the parts aren't very good.[14]

Gehry's fragmentation of what could have been a single mass into separate elements is a form of miniaturization that implies an accretion of houses, a social settlement. He is creating an apparent communal aggregation where none exists. Yet he is also careful not to become too literal. Discussing an early version of the Santa Monica house in an interview conducted by Martin Filler for a profile in *Art in America,* Gehry said: "I . . . changed it because it was looking too much like a village, and I wanted the building not to look like buildings. I wanted to give them a different kind of objecthood."[15] Just as artists in the nineteenth century represented nature with meticulous care at the very time when industrialization was beginning to threaten its very existence, so Gehry's buildings masquerading as Potemkin villages may be a protective gesture against our unfocused urban environment. His Wosk Residence, Beverly Hills (1982-1984), and his Winton Guest House,

13. *Beyond Utopia, op. cit.,* p 53.
14. *Ibid.,* pp 53-54.
15. Martin Filler, "Eccentric Space: Frank Gehry," *Art in America,* June 1980, p 114.

Wayzata, Minnesota (1983-1986), the already mentioned Cabrillo Marine Museum, Loyola Law School, and the recently completed California Aerospace Museum, Los Angeles (1982-1984) are all characteristic examples of this kind of fractured composition.

The urge to create a locus, a sense of place, in the face of urban and suburban sprawl has also been evident in a number of early works by Charles Moore, in particular in the house he designed for himself at Orinda, California (1962). Here two canopies, like baldachinos, are inserted into the interior of the house to produce a feeling of intimate spaces within an otherwise open interior. In his Sea Ranch Condominium I, California (1963-1966) Moore has clustered apartment units around an open court in such a fashion as to suggest a small town in the manner of Alvar Aalto's Säynätsalo Town Center, Finland (1950-1952). Inside Moore's own house, a baldachino (here with a sleeping loft on top) marks off a "protected" conversation zone within a two-story space. Moore has spoken about the baldachino and other miniaturized architectural forms, such as aediculae, as markers of a sacred space in both a religious and domestic context.

Because the family no longer provides a real emotional center, the architecture is called on to perform double duty: to create the image of a safe haven. Where Moore more often responds by subdividing an interior space, Gehry's fragmentation of forms is more thoroughgoing. In fact, in most of Gehry's recent works in which this method is applied, the older disjunction between metallic exterior and wooden interior as it had been used in the Davis Studio and Gehry's Santa Monica house, is no longer expressed quite as blatantly. It is as if the fracturing of the building mass has become a substitute for the hard shell-soft core composition of the earlier designs.

In a step much more flagrant than either Moore's or Gehry's form of miniaturization, Michael Graves had proposed an allusion to the small-scale village in the context of a large public building. In his Portland Building, Portland, Oregon (1982), an administrative extension of Portland's City Hall, Graves projected a series of small pavilions for its rooftop. This element of the design was not approved by the client, however. Had it been executed, the miniature village, consisting of a series of small temples and architectural follies, would have been visible only to office workers in nearby higher buildings. Though this arrangement might have been entertaining for onlookers from above, such an architectural playground would also have been oddly retrospective rather than meaningful for present conditions. There is something incongruous about a sacred temple precinct on top of a modern office building. Gehry's type of fractured assemblages, on the other hand, constitute an appropriately disquieting response to fragmentation of the extended family, community and urban space.

Gehry's reconstitution of screen walls, whether of corrugated metal, plywood, or any other material, into three-dimensional structures parallels other tendencies in contemporary architecture in America. For instance, Robert Venturi has taken as his archetypal models the advertising billboard, and what he and his partner, Denise Scott Brown, have called the "decorated shed." The commercial roadside building with a strongly defined, billboardlike facade and a "dumb" enclosure, has in effect reduced our normal conception of architectural definition to a planar screen to which the contained space seems attached almost as an afterthought. The facade is the carrier of significant design gestures, while the container on its three remaining sides is expressed as an ordinary object, thereby stressing the separateness of the facade from the building.[16]

In some of the larger works of Charles Moore, comparable effects are achieved through more theatrical, scenographic devices. In his Kresge College, Santa Cruz, California (1973), or the more recent Piazza d'Italia, New Orleans (1979), a narrow, layered space is created by means of exaggerated facades that function like stage sets. In the modernist work of Richard Meier, screenlike effects are often used to define the building behind. On the exterior, thus, space is not made corporeal through thick walls or deep reveals, but appears trapped in the narrow channel between screen wall and the building proper, as in his Hartford Seminary, Hartford, Connecticut (1978-1981), or his Museum of Decorative Arts, Frankfurt (1979-1985). In Peter Eisenman's abstruse residential houses, intended as equivalents of mental constructs, architectural space consists of complex, densely interwoven slots. In some of John Hejduk's abstract projects the notion of containing wall surrounding an interior has been literally turned inside-out. A gigantic wall marks the space like some ceremonial stele, and rooms are attached to it as separate elements. The older notion of a fully animated Baroque "Raum" or even the continuous, flowing interiors of the early modern movement are rarely employed today by either modernists or postmodernists. Instead, architectural space is thin, layered and constricted. Quite unlike a characteristically generous Baroque space, compressed layers suggest withdrawal from our natural environment into a space that can be as exciting as it is tension-provoking. The critic Kenneth Frampton has referred to Frank Gehry's architecture as "subversive" and "anti-architecture."[17] This is undoubtedly true if we take architecture of earlier periods as our measuring stick. However, every age has to redefine the notion of architectural expression and space. The soft forms of French Art Nouveau are subversive and anti-architectural if we take as the norm a Beaux-Arts Classicism. The volumetric spaces enclosed by the thinnest of walls typical of the International Style might strike us as anti-architectural if we compare them to the massive, sculptural exteriors of the Baroque period. While the thrown-together look of Gehry's buildings is unique, the implications of his definition of form and space are part of a current redefinition of our social space.

16. Rosemarie Haag Bletter, "Transformations of the American Vernacular: The Work of Venturi, Rauch, & Scott Brown," *Venturi, Rauch and Scott Brown: A Generation of Architecture,* exhibition catalogue, Krannert Art Museum, University of Illinois at Urbana-Champaign, 1984, pp 2-19.
17. Martin Filler, "Eccentric Space: Frank Gehry," *op. cit.,* p 114.
18. *Beyond Utopia, op. cit.,* p 50.
19. Rosemarie Haag Bletter, "Kurt Schwitters' Unfinished Rooms," *Progressive Architecture,* September 1977, pp 97-99.

The "Blue Window" from
Kurt Schwitters's *Merzbau.*
Photographed 1933.

Gehry's protective metallic exteriors, fragmentation of massing, internalization of public space, and employment of screen walls suggesting forced perspective but inspired by abstract art rather than theatrical illusion, all reinforce a sense of withdrawal from the public realm. Gehry himself may not entirely agree with this assessment. His response to architectural problems is always sensibly low-key instead of theoretical. He even feigns guileless naiveté, though he is never anti-intellectual. His reactions are intuitive, not fitted into an ideological program. His explanation of spatial fragmentation in the Loyola Law School, cited before, deals forthrightly with the larger issue of urban context, but when he discusses a similar design procedure in the Norton House, Venice, California (1983-1984), his justification is at the same time quite pragmatic:

What I like doing best is breaking down the project into as many separate parts as possible. . . . So, instead of a house being one thing, it's ten things. It allows the client more involvement, because you can say, 'Well, I've got ten images now that are going to compose your house. Those images can relate to all kinds of symbolic things, ideas that you've liked, places you've liked, bits and pieces of your life that you would like to recall.' I think in terms of involving the client . . .[18]

The apparent unruly randomness of Gehry's designs springs first of all from his immediate responses to textures, materials and setting. His continuing intense curiosity about contemporary art and his recent collaborations with the artists Richard Serra and Claes Oldenburg have kept him from falling into a formulaic approach to architecture. He assembles "found" materials in the way Antonio Gaudi experimented with burnt bricks, broken dishes, and metal ornaments from sewing machines. At the same time Gehry gives shape to shadows lurking beneath the surface of our culture. His interest in assigning symbolic, mnemonic values to elements of a design suggests the need for a continually changing expression as in Kurt Schwitters's *Merzbau.*

Begun around 1923, the *Merzbau* grew over the next decade from a small sculptural experiment into a cavernous interior. As the mad structure continually took on new forms, Schwitters, in the spirit of Dada and Expressionism, created an unmeasurable, forever unfinished space, and the first lived-in environmental sculpture.[19] Schwitters's sculpture gradually grew from inside out to absorb the old house, whereas Gehry, the architect, works from the outside in by entrapping the original bungalow of his Santa Monica house within a new shell.

Gehry decomposes and simultaneously reconstructs space. Both procedures coexist in a state of tension. If he is neither a modernist nor a postmodernist, we might call him the first synthetic constructivist. The relationship in his work between the artist's abstracted perspectival illusions and three-dimensional architecture creates something of a paradox. But in the end the painter's artifice is turned into a meaningful architectural edifice.

Jung Institute 1976
Los Angeles, California

The Jung Institute provided an opportunity to
test the idea of using the shell from the Ron
Davis Studio as a starting point, and say to the
Jung analysts, who had diverse needs, that
each department of the Institute could move
into one of these shapes, and adapt themselves to it. That freed me from varying the
shapes, because it said that diverse
experiences would create a variety of responses from the users.

This is a very small study. We were hired
to do an exploratory study and so there wasn't
any money to detail it. The site was in an
industrial area of Los Angeles. It was a
mishmash of tiltups [precast concrete walls],
parking lots and power lines. There wasn't
much to look at, so I took the idea we started
with at Cochiti Lake in the desert, where you
create a zone that's yours within the chaos.

We decided to build twelve-foot walls
around the site and put objects inside. Interest
in the sky then became quite strong. When you
perceive an edge, the sky gets closer to you;
it's an incredible phenomenon. All of a sudden
you feel like you're in it rather than looking at
it. That sense of connecting with the sky, just
by free association, led me to water and the
idea of taking the parking lot aesthetic and
hot-mopping it [with black asphalt], so that it
would hold a couple of inches of water. It
wouldn't hold a lot, but it would be enough to
create a pool that would be very reflective
because of the asphalt.

I found out after my dealings with the Jung
Institute how strong a symbol water was for
Jung—a symbol of the unconscious. I never
remember if I knew that before or after, but I
don't remember knowing it before. That idea,
the water trick, is being done for the first time
at the Hollywood Library. The Danziger Studio
and the Jung Institute are in the Hollywood
Library, plus a few new ones.

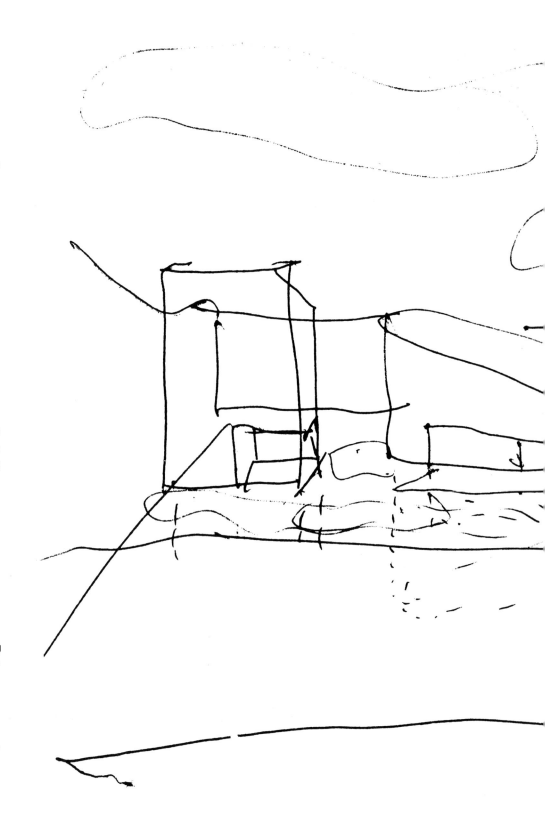

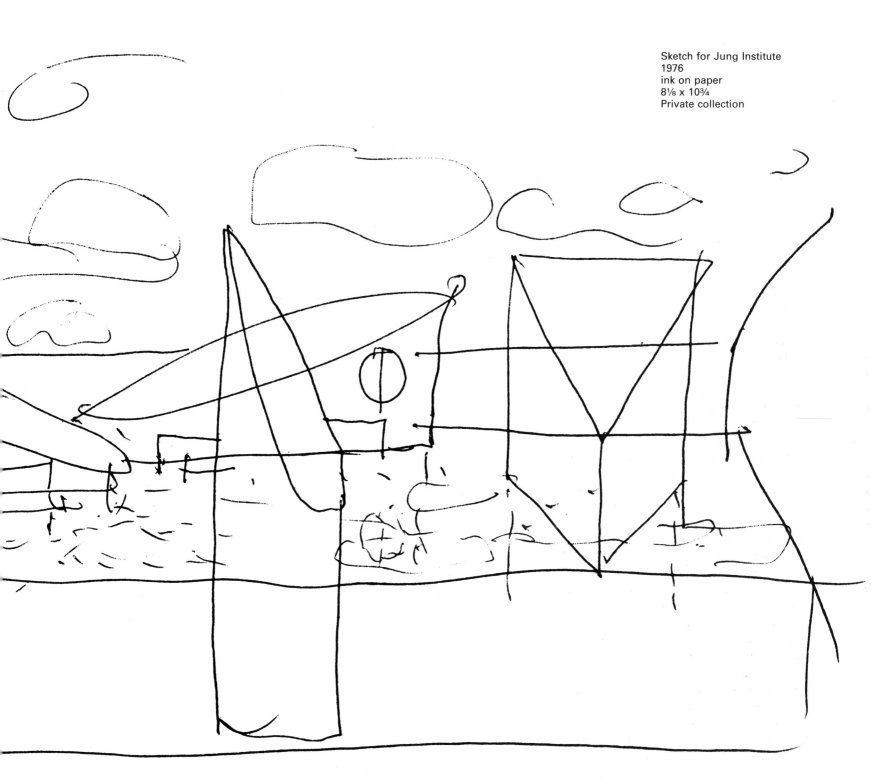

Sketch for Jung Institute
1976
ink on paper
8⅛ x 10¾
Private collection

Gunther House   1978
Encinal Bluffs, California

The Gunther House preceded the Wagner and Familian houses. It was the beginning of my use of chain link. One of the key words the client told me when he started this house was that he was only going to use it on weekends and he wanted it to be secure during the week. So naturally the word secure suggested the words chain link and I was really fascinated with it. Again, it was like the cardboard; it was

a material there was so much denial about. People used it in great quantities, and yet the denial syndrome was great. When you talk about using chain link people are filled with horror. But if they have a chain link fence around their house and you ask, 'Why aren't you filled with horror about that?' they say, 'Oh, that's just a fence.' Somehow there's the idea that if it's inevitable it's OK, but if it's a

Gunther House model, west
(opposite) and south
elevations.

conscious or intentional use of the material, it's somehow threatening. I really got interested in that idea. When I went to the chain-link manufacturers to ask them for information about the material, they said, 'Listen, we sell more of this stuff than we need to, and we're not looking for new ideas.' That was the same kind of response I had gotten from the cardboard company. Those responses interest me a lot. So that's why chain link started. In this study I made complete forms of chain link, with forms inside the forms, so that the shadow patterns of the forms inside the forms played against the very simple box of the house.

**Wagner House   1978
Malibu, California**

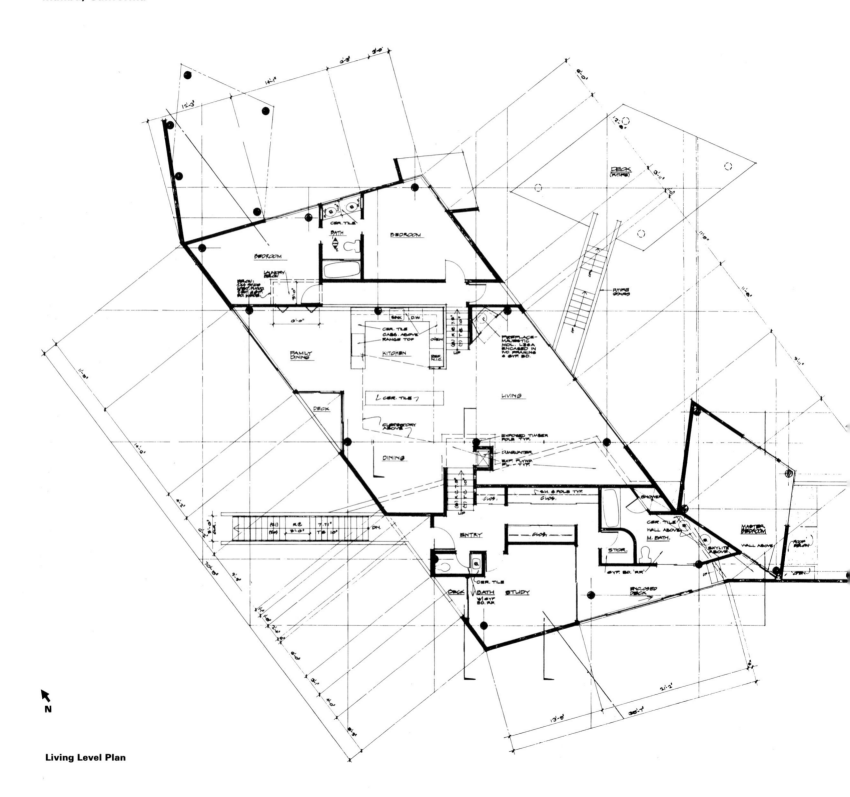

N

Living Level Plan

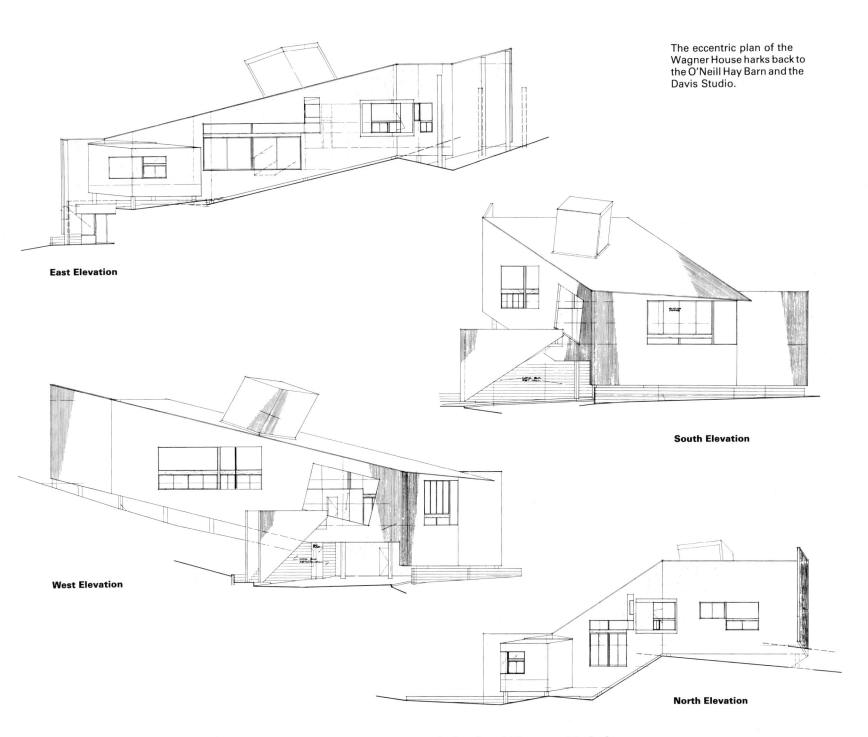

East Elevation

The eccentric plan of the Wagner House harks back to the O'Neill Hay Barn and the Davis Studio.

South Elevation

West Elevation

North Elevation

The Wagner House was a continuation of the Ron Davis project in terms of the materials used. In this case the site was very demanding. It was a slope, and the client insisted that we not touch the slope, for environmental reasons. How do you build a house on a slope and not touch the slope? That was kind of a trick. We supported it on the least expensive construction I could find. We used telephone pole technology and floated a boxlike object above the slope.

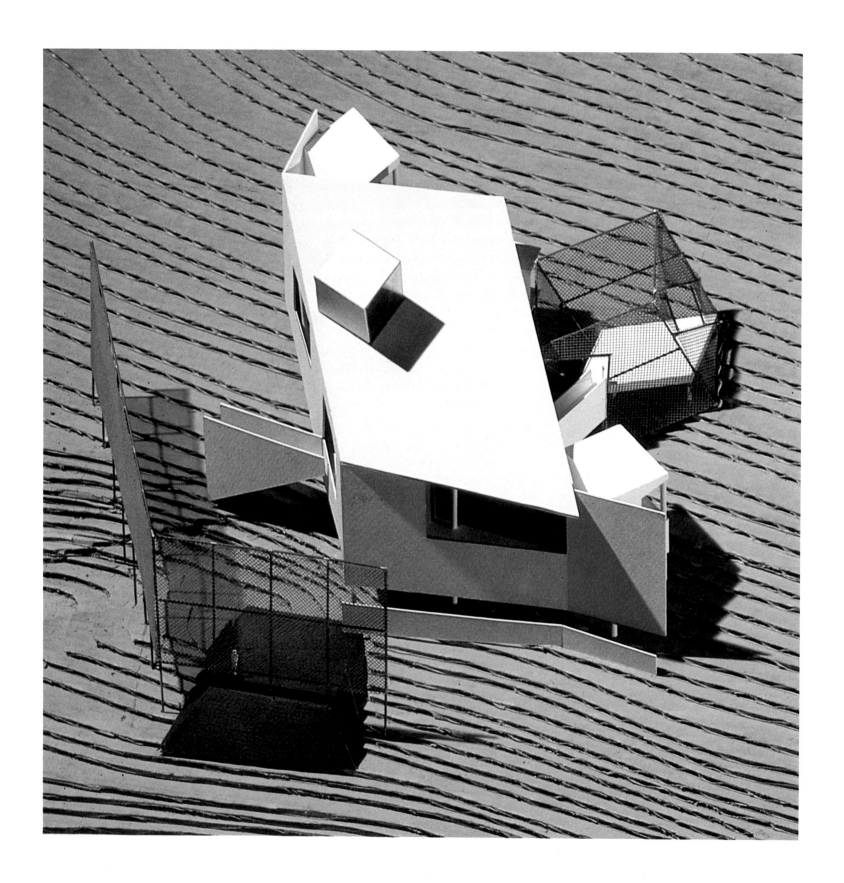

Wagner House

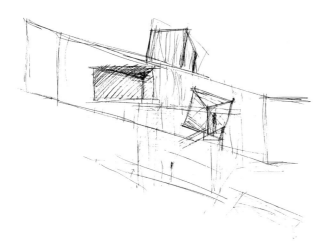

Sketch for Wagner
House   1978
ink on paper
8⅛ x 10¾
Collection the architect

This powerful sketch of
proposed windows indicates
the direction Gehry would
follow in several unrealized
projects of 1978. A cubistic
window was finally achieved
in his own house (p 34).

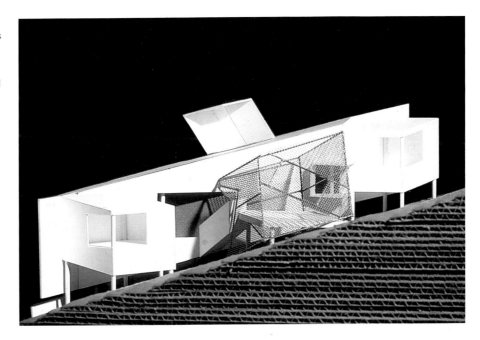

**I drew the building as an axonometric in
real space, so that when you looked at it you'd
click it into a box, a right-angled box, rather
than a parallelepiped. I wanted it to look like
the box was precariously perched on the
hillside, almost sliding down. That was one
idea. The other was to place chain link, which
I'd started playing with by then, into
juxtaposition with corrugated metal, because
when you put chain link in front of corrugated
metal, the corrugated metal glistens in
sunlight.**

The Wagner model, east
(top) and west elevations.

(opposite)
Bird's-eye view of the model
for the Wagner House.

Familian House   1978
Santa Monica, California

This was a house for an art collector. It was an attempt to make a simple container very simple by cutting into it with windows in raw framing, the kind of balloon framing that housing is made of in Los Angeles. I was interested in the immediacy of the raw framing before it was covered up. It had a quality that paintings have, like a brushstroke that's just been placed. How do you get that quality into a building?

Most frame buildings look great under construction, but when they're covered they look like hell. So I was trying to capitalize on that, and see if there wasn't a way to capture the good side of the equation. That was the thrust of the Familian House, to play with that immediacy and see if it could be put under glass somehow. The ideas that were started there were used in my house, in the Gemini Studio and in the Spiller House. The idea still appears as part of my vocabulary in the Norton House.

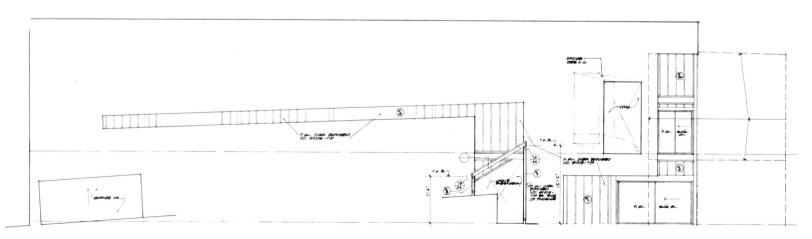

North Elevation

For the Familian House, as in the Gunther and Wagner projects, Gehry proposed exposing the structural framework. In this plan we see the separation of functional elements into distinct units, a characteristic of the built work of the early 1980s in such projects as the Benson House (p 118).

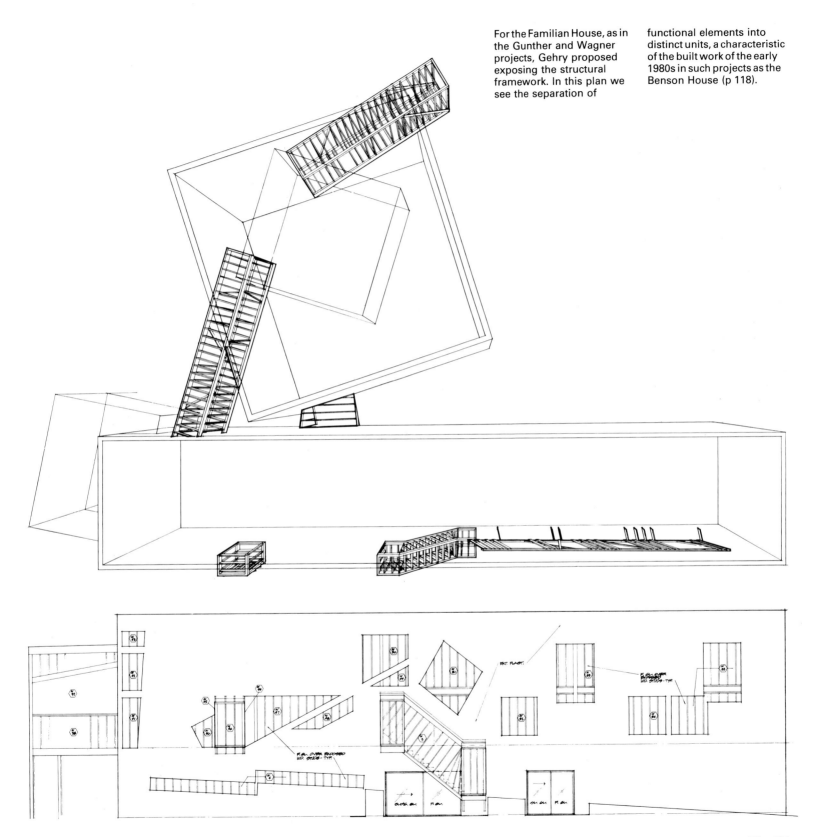

South Elevation

De Menil House   1978
New York City

The de Menil renovation came after my own house. The design presented to the client and initially approved was a complete renovation of the interior. We decided to leave the exterior shell, tear out everything in the interior and build completely new inside. The program, requiring essentially two apartments, one for mama and one for daughter, led me to the idea of building two separate buildings inside the space, which was a reverse of my house where I built a new house around the existing structure.

The models and sketches show the way I proposed to float new space above a step-down garden that was the joint living

This project for a New York City brownstone was never completely carried out as Gehry envisioned it. Views of the model and Gehry's comments indicate the direction he was taking. The existing building is shown opposite (left).

space. This also allowed for a garage, a lower-level kitchen, servants' quarters and a swimming pool-recreation room. At some moment my client decided not to do it, and with much pain in my heart I helped her with a lesser remodeling in which the building was left intact and just some of the rooms were moved around, with the idea of getting this one behind us and continuing on a new project for the family. But we never got it behind us and never did a new project. What we actually did has gone through many iterations.

Since I worked on it, the building has been changed by Doug Wheeler and other artists; it was an interesting continuum. It fits my original idea, which was to have the late Gordon Matta-Clark do the demolition and then work against it. I would have loved that.

Mid-Atlantic Toyota 1978
Glen Burnie, Maryland

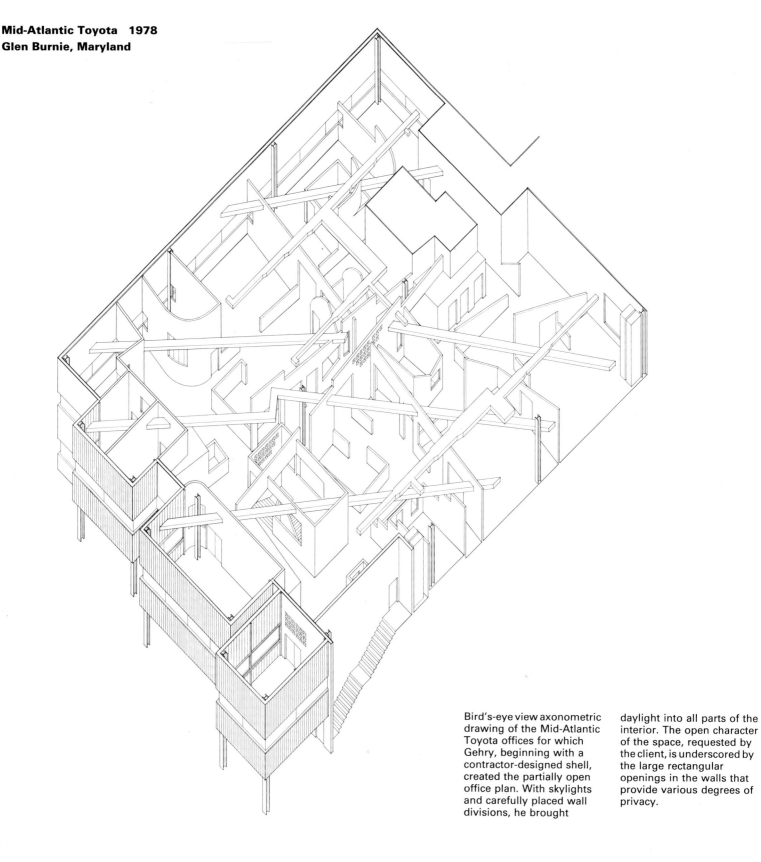

Bird's-eye view axonometric drawing of the Mid-Atlantic Toyota offices for which Gehry, beginning with a contractor-designed shell, created the partially open office plan. With skylights and carefully placed wall divisions, he brought daylight into all parts of the interior. The open character of the space, requested by the client, is underscored by the large rectangular openings in the walls that provide various degrees of privacy.

Mid-Atlantic Toyota is an extension of the interiors system idea started at Rouse, but it is more individualistic and uses cheaper materials. Simple, Sheetrock walls are combined with continuing work on indirect lighting.

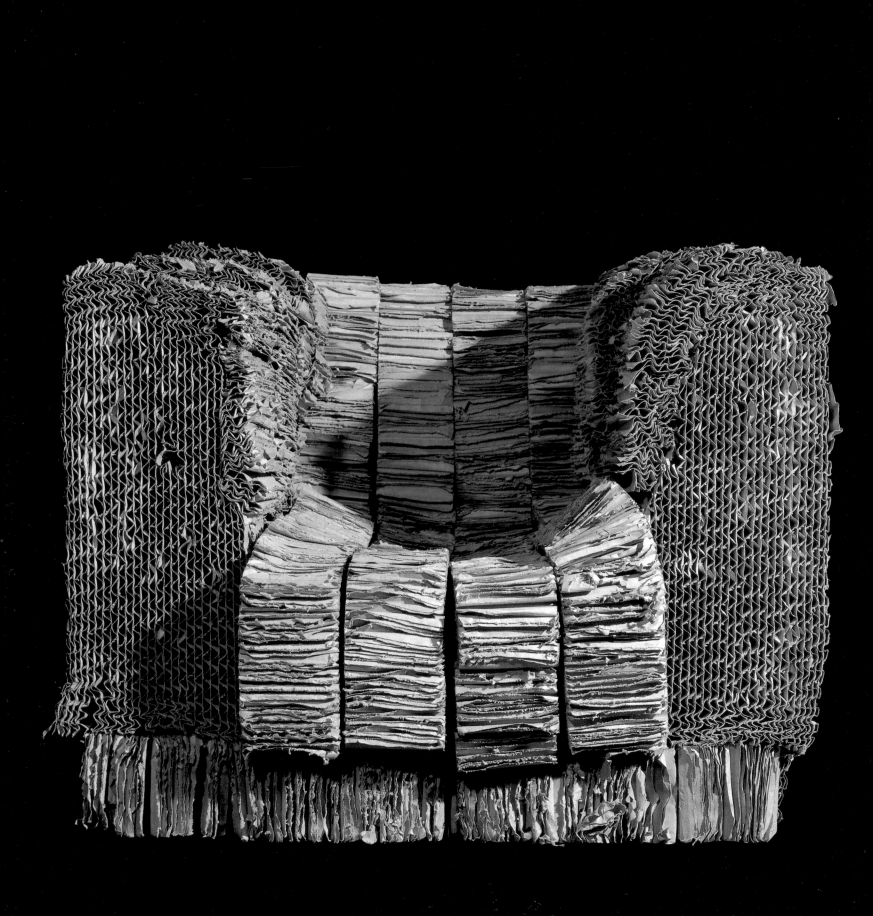

Joseph Giovannini

Edges, Easy and Experimental

Experimental Edges
Armchair 1980
laminated, corrugated
cardboard
37 x 46 x 40
Collection the architect

In the furniture series
Experimental Edges,
1979-1986, Gehry explored a
more flamboyant approach
to cardboard than he had
used in the earlier Easy
Edges group (pp 68, 69).

It was his furniture, not his buildings, that first brought Frank Gehry national attention. In 1972, the seventeen cardboard pieces in the Easy Edges line appeared in most major newspapers and in prominent department stores. In his career of otherwise very reasonable designs, they were among the first works to immediately capture the attention of the viewer. The corrugated cardboard was charming, abrasive and unexpected: a throwaway material had been transformed into charismatic furniture suitable for most American houses. These pieces were the first of many arresting designs to follow.

If the furniture attracted attention, it also sustained it—hardly one-liners, the pieces had layers of messages. The cardboard projected the wholesome connotations of corduroy or wood, and was in fact stained, joined and generally worked as wood. Three of the chairs could even hold up a car, as one publicity shot demonstrated. In profile, some of the pieces looked like vigorous line drawings; others, like the wiggle side chair and the stand-up bar, seem to have been slowly poured. They had spirit and humor, and projected the teasing sense that the designer had gotten away with something. The line promised to be the Volkswagen of furniture, bringing good design to a mass market. The dining chair, for example, which cost seven dollars to manufacture in 1972, retailed for only thirty-seven dollars.

The pieces had wide appeal. Gehry, who haunted the showrooms, found one woman buying a pair of chairs for the antique table in her breakfast room. He also received letters from people like Edward Logue of the Urban Development Corporation in New York, who was interested in the furniture's applicability to public housing. Chuck Dietrich of California's Synanon also expressed interest, as he was looking both for projects members of the halfway house could do themselves, and for furniture for the organization's buildings.

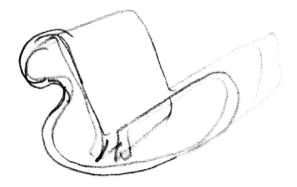

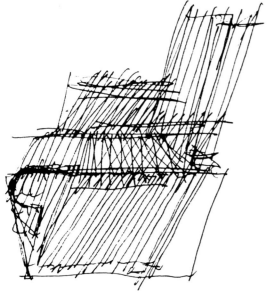

But abruptly, after only three months on the market, and as sales peaked, Gehry withdrew the line: "I started to feel threatened; I locked myself into a room for weeks to question my life. I decided I'm an architect, not a furniture designer. I'm not going to go that way. I called a halt."

Gehry, who held the patent on the furniture, collapsed the enterprise and recommitted himself to architecture, and within a decade firmly established himself as one of the leading American architects of his generation. Despite the subsequent emphasis on architecture, Gehry has returned frequently to furniture and especially to cardboard. He later produced the less commercial Experimental Edges pieces, which briefly became a gallery item, and then reissued Easy Edges in 1982, at the request of Bloomingdale's. He is currently working with a European firm on yet another variation of the corrugated furniture—this time in plastic.

Like the Gropius chair, the Morris chair, the Mackintosh chair, Gehry's cardboard furniture captures much of the character and message of his other work, embodying in its evolution his developing architectural concerns. As is typical of Gehry, he has chosen in his furniture to work with a "difficult" material—one with the connotation of cheapness and the look of rawness. The alchemy of transforming a "dismissable" material into "design" may seem like an effortless transformation, given the results, but the ease is only apparent. The designs are highly studied and refined; the final subtlety is that the rawness remains intact, that it has been worked on but not polished. In the case of the furniture, there is a sense of the real cardboard and not of any surface finish. "Even though I often put as much detail work into what I do as anyone, it always appears casual. That's the edge I'm after," he has said. As in much of the work, the Easy Edges pieces had an underlying implication of social responsibility: Gehry had delivered good design at an accessible price.

In the progression from Easy Edges to Experimental Edges, there was also Gehry's own migration from Bloomingdale's to the Max Protetch Gallery, and his vacillation between a political liberalism and the elitism of the art world. Easy Edges was overwhelmingly commercial and, despite the intentional rawness of the material, slickly marketed—one brochure lists its acoustic properties as a selling point. Its clean-looking image was emphasized in photographs: the line might, it was hoped, reach deeply into the middle class. But in its next incarnation, Experimental Edges, the notion of function, acoustic or otherwise, had dropped out. "I was trying to do something that was not marketable," he says. It became a gallery object—still a cheap material, but sold as art.

The vector of his imagination and that of his furniture and architecture is finally not to the department store or, like so many Eames chairs, to every airport in the land, but to the rarefied art world and the art

Easy Edges High Chair   1972
corrugated cardboard
and pressed fiber
45 x 28 x 12
Collection Joan and Jack Quinn

patron. This is perhaps inevitable since Gehry's own design method—he is preoccupied with process—resembles more that of the artist, who works with materials "hands-on," than that of the architect, who problem-solves on paper, "hands-off."

"We always designed furniture," he says, recalling with characteristic self-deprecation that the first furniture he made was a collapsible latrine when he served in the army. Educated as an architect at the University of Southern California, he was assigned to Fort Benning, Georgia. "They tested my mettle by having me design knock-down furniture—a field latrine." For the company's dayrooms—where soldiers phoned, wrote letters and mingled—he designed an interior with wood elements that was "very Frank Lloyd Wright—columns with outriggers that had uplights," he says.

"When you are out of architecture school in California, you have a very strong Japanese influence." The architect who was to become famous for designing buildings that made a virtue out of the demise of craft, then, actually started with forms that were steeped in a craft tradition. The renovation of the offices of Faith Plating in Los Angeles, for example, in 1964, featured finely crafted teak and oak, beautifully finished to reveal their grains. "I learned all that from Rudy Baumfeld (a partner) in the Gruen office—we inherited his craftsman." At Faith Plating, there was wood banding at the top and bottom of the perimeter walls; in the conference room, the table rested on a broad wood ledge; there were sliding shoji doors. The furniture was part of the architecture and was environmental, and had not yet come away from the building to occupy space as an isolated object. "It had a Japanese sense of materiality," he says, adding that it was also in the spirit of Danish modern furniture of the 1950s, like that of Hans Wegner.

In 1968 the Gehry office worked on the Joseph Magnin department stores in Costa Mesa and San José, and though the jobs remain among a number of background projects, two ideas seeded in them would grow to greater significance for the office. One was to clear the ceiling of vents and lighting fixtures so that the merchandise would stand out. Consequently, like the merchandise, the store fixtures Gehry designed also stood out more as objects within the space. The second idea was the investigation of cardboard as a material for furniture.

The architects hired Don Chadwick, who was later to create furniture for Herman Miller, to design some cardboard pieces. "We started looking at cardboard; it must have been in the air," says Gehry. He describes the furniture that resulted as the sort an engineer would produce: "It was folded for strength, done in the obvious way. It was very effective, flat surfaced." In profile, the pieces were like park benches, with cardboard slats bent in an upside-down U inserted in the structure; the

In two projects for the Joseph Magnin stores, Gehry created a flexible environment for the display of merchandise, using indirect lighting, movable partitions and counters constructed of inexpensive materials, which can be reorganized with ease.

Joseph Magnin Stores 1968
Costa Mesa and San José, California

I'd worked on stores for Joseph Magnin when I was at Victor Gruen. I was concerned about the kind of money that was spent on the details of teak and oak and special glass and light fixtures versus the problem I saw of a retail outlet having to respond to the very, very capricious fashion market. It bothered me to see this kind of static building type: it may not have been the architecture, but the way materials were used. I can imagine now using such materials but in a different way.

When I got to the Magnin store I was interested in getting rid of all those expensive materials, making a stage set, making a theater for selling clothes. I began with the lighting. The normal down lighting in department stores is very disturbing, as are all the diffusers and all the junk on the ceiling. I wanted indirect lighting because I didn't want to see the light fixtures. I wanted the space to be lit like a volume. I felt that I wanted to create a strong neutral space, a backdrop, even though I thought the architecture of the forms could be complicated as long as it was of a different scale from the merchandise or the people. Getting rid of all those things helped me change the scale. Architecture became a background and the merchandise really stood out in this store.

folds gave the furniture structural rigidity. Gehry himself remained somewhat peripheral to this effort, though the idea to work with cardboard was his, and the effort was the start of his long involvement with cardboard. Gehry proved not to be interested in the engineering of the material.

He recalls one day in 1968 staring at the contour of a cardboard site model that was in the office. "I was just looking and looking at it, and I had an idea." The idea was to cut profiles of furniture out of individual sheets of cardboard and to layer the pieces into a monolithic piece of furniture, just as the contour model had been built up by layering cardboard.

Gehry hired Josh Young, an artist and former student of his friend, the artist Robert Irwin, to research cardboard for its strengths, sizes, workability, cost and availability. "You always research a material completely—an artist cuts it, works with it. I had learned this from the artists I knew."

Gehry still has the first piece he designed—the long, sturdy, matter of fact desk in his office, which Young built. "Everyone looked at it and called it corduroy cardboard." The sides of the desk exposed strata of the cardboard, and the top was simply a white plastic laminate surface. "It's overkill," he says referring to its strength. After the desk, he and Young made a file cabinet—a rectangular table of cardboard with walls two inches thick, and metal channels for the drawers mounted on the sides. "I stood on it without drawers in it, and John and I realized it was much stronger than anyone had expected. It was like a beam." In the conference room of the office, there is also a four-by-twelve foot cardboard table dating from about this time, and Gehry, talking informally, sits on its edge unself-consciously, as he has done hundreds of times, confident that the furniture can support him.

Like plywood, which is made of thin sheets of wood laminated so that the grain of each sheet alternates direction, the furniture was built up of cardboard sheets stacked so that the fluting inside each was ninety degrees off that of the sheets immediately above and below. The Gehry firm found that the sheets could be die-cut inexpensively. The profile for a piece of furniture could be punched out of a sheet of cardboard, and a number of dies could be cut out of the same sheet. The one-ply sheets, with glue on each side, were stacked into a jig until they were deep enough to form the width of the piece of furniture—a process that took about one minute per piece of furniture. Thin metal dowels were placed where necessary. For example, double dowels were inserted at the bottom of the chairs, serving as castors and giving the bottom strength.

On 15 May 1972, Frank O. Gehry, as inventor, applied for and received U.S. Patent No. 4,067,615. The abstract reads, in part:

Cardboard Furniture   ongoing since 1969

Cardboard furniture. What an albatross. Boy did I get myself in trouble with this one! It grew out of the Magnin stores and the need to find something cheap and disposable for fixtures. I started experimenting with cardboard in all the ways one would think of it in terms of efficiency; folded sheets make a structure very economically. Somehow, when you made something, it wasn't very nice. It was folded cardboard. Then one day I was looking at architectural contour models, which were layers of cardboard. I was looking at the end elevation with its combed look, and I got excited about it. I started to see it as an aesthetic opportunity, and I made the desk I still use. I didn't think of going beyond that.

An article of furniture or other similar load-bearing structural article comprises a laminate of flat, corrugated, cardboard pieces conforming generally to the cross-sectional shape of the article. The plane of each piece is generally parallel to the direction in which the load is predominantly applied with the flutes of adjacent corrugated cardboard pieces extending at right angles to each other. The individual pieces are secured together adhesively and, if desired, support stringers and end pieces may be used for increased rigidity and, thus, improved stability.

With this furniture Gehry had designed a freestanding object that involved no craft, and required only the simplest of industrial, assembly-line processes. The furniture had nothing to do with the Frank Lloyd Wright or Japanese-inspired "environmental" furniture that was part of a building. It was very different in nature, too, from the Eames furniture so carefully prototyped in Venice, near Gehry's office. The Gehry furniture as presented on the market was clever, perhaps facile, and faintly humorous. As he was then doing with corrugated metal in the Ron Davis Studio, and was later to do with chain-link fencing and plywood, Gehry had recoded an everyday material, giving it vastly different connotations.

Brilliant though the cardboard furniture was, Gehry's interest in it flagged. "I had exhausted its potential; I was finished. I was going on to something else."

However, Robert Irwin encouraged him to continue developing it, and came in with drawings of a possible chair. "It freaked me out that he was co-opting my stuff and I became competitive. I started designing furiously." Irwin brought in Jack Brogan, a craftsman and "tech guy," according to Gehry, to further develop the idea. Brogan would take a simple sketch, blow it up photostatically, and produce the piece by the next day.

"It was Irwin who egged me on—his energy and excitement about this pulled it off." Gehry credits Irwin with having generated the basic idea for the armchair; the wiggle stool, he says, was a collaboration. Other pieces included an R-shaped bar stool and a roughly C-shaped rocker, as well as nesting tables and chairs and stacking shelves. The approach had enormous design potential. Some pieces in the line, like the chaise longue, played on traditional furniture types, so that the furniture seemed original within recognized conventions. There was, too, careful control over image. All the pieces were likable; none were abrasive. Those with a quiet oddness were not commercially produced.

Richard Salomon, a New York entrepreneur who had promoted Yves Saint Laurent and Vidal Sassoon, learned of the furniture and bought into the project, insisting that the artist be highly visible in the enterprise. Like YSL and Sassoon, Gehry would be personally identified with the product. For Gehry, the task of being the visible designer soon became onerous. He had to spend increasing amounts of time in business meetings, and devoted about a year to bringing out the furniture

Easy Edges Rocker 1971
laminated, corrugated
cardboard
32 inches high. Mfr.: Easy
Edges
Collection The Museum of
Modern Art, New York
Gift of the manufacturer

(below)
Easy Edges Table and
Chairs 1982
laminated, corrugated
cardboard
table: 32 x 84 x 36
chair: 33½ x 18½ x 15½
Collection Bruce and
Rebecca Marder

(opposite)
Easy Edges Wiggle Side
Chair 1970
laminated, corrugated
cardboard
38⅜ x 14¼
Collection Keith Berwick

Cardboard Furniture   ongoing since 1969

But once it was built I became fascinated with how it could be made lighter, because it was so heavy. So we started cutting away at it and thinking, 'How much more can we cut away before this thing falls, and what kinds of things can we make?'

We made a file cabinet, a table and a desk. They all worked fabulously. I made those three pieces and thought, 'That's great, it works, go on and do something else.' Then Robert Irwin came along and started making funny drawings, and I was involved. We were making shapes, working with spring, and with the resiliency of the paper; we were interested in all aspects of the paper. The material research on this was thorough. We did fire testing, color testing, lamination testing, we varied the strengths. We went at it very scientifically. By the time we had gone into production we were quite knowledgeable about the paper and its strength. For instance just dyeing the paper reduced the strength by twenty percent. So if you went to colors you'd have to redesign. There were a lot of nuances. We explored different kinds of shapes. The thing that came out as Easy Edges was the most economical at that time to make, because we were able to tie into the process of making corrugated paper and get the die-cutting done as part of the paper order. We developed a whole assembly-line technology.

Experimental Edges Chaise Longue 1980
laminated, corrugated cardboard
34 x 42 x 93
Courtesy New City Editions

(below)
Experimental Edges Rocker 1980
laminated, corrugated cardboard
31 x 35 x 53
Collection the architect

It's fascinating to work with a material that has resiliency and that keeps its form. The aesthetic qualities of it were very special because it looked like corduroy, it felt like corduroy, it was seductive. It was warm and it could be used in a variety of settings—it was a neutral kind of material. We experimented with all kinds of things and endless shapes. We focused on the ribbon form for Easy Edges because it was the cheapest system to produce. But we also made furniture that looked like architectural contour models. We made blocks that looked like Stonehenge. You could put them together, glue them like rocks and make strange, cactuslike furniture. We tried colors, we changed colors, we tried striped furniture. The furniture was striped because of color changes in the core. We played with a lot of things that nobody's ever seen. We also found out that the cardboard reacted like wood. If you painted it, it was no longer that warm stuff, it became sort of rigid. But if you used wood stains, you carried the character of the material through. We were able to use all the wood stains. That also was never publicly shown.

I carried the ideas of resiliency beyond that and got into wider flutes. These were resilient, but they didn't come back as completely as the Easy Edges material. It was something I tabled and didn't go back to until 1969. There was another thing I always wanted to go back to and I still haven't: taking the cardboard furniture as we made it and turning it ninety degrees. Now you're sitting on the board, but with its dense honeycomb it has bounce, and you can regulate that. I think there's a middle ground there that I would like to explore.

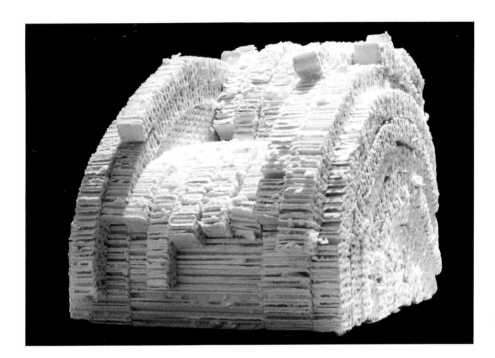

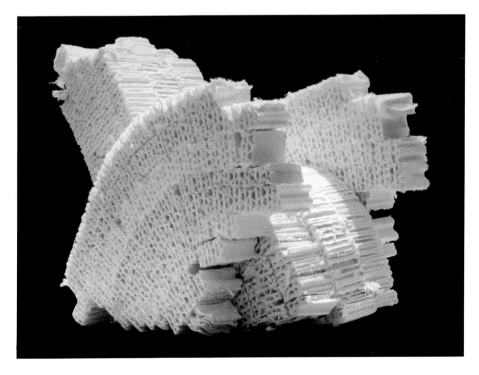

Models for Experimental
Edges   1985

The Rouse Company Headquarters   1974
Columbia, Maryland

The Rouse Company Headquarters was a very early demonstration of the potential for flexibility in the partially open plan, which has become a given in today's computerized office environment.

The Rouse Company was a developer-client whose principles were very easy for me to support. They were the first developer that gave me good-sized work to do, so I felt a very strong personal relationship with them. Jim Rouse is a brilliant man—he's incredible to talk with. We did several projects for them and then we were given the headquarters building. I got interested in two aspects of the building: the exterior or sculptural quality of the building in relation to the site, and thinking of it as a container; and then the interiors, thought of as a system.

I joined the interiors with the air conditioning, heating, lighting and electrical distribution. I saw them as one thing. I think that is a little bit different from the way buildings are thought of by most people. We used this job as a way to design the exterior and interior as separate elements. I was very interested in an inexpensive shell whose edges, rather than finished and sculpturally complete, would be ragged, so that connecting to it would be easy. It would be an indeterminate exterior.

The Rouse building exterior is as open as its interior, stacking up to create a central light-filled atrium at its core.

On the inside we started analyzing various mechanical and lighting systems—of course I wanted to use indirect light—and floor distribution systems. We started doing research on computer floors and helped develop a way of making carpet tiles for them. Up to that point only asphalt tile and linoleum were in use. So this was one of the first applications of the computer floor for general office use, not just for computer rooms. We experimented with that, we experimented with the lighting, we built mock-ups in our office of the lighting. We built work stations, tested them and developed the whole work station system. In effect, it was a criticism of Knoll and Herman Miller, who at that time had their work stations all at one height. I was trying to break that down, and I learned from the Magnin stores that just to build in flexibility wasn't enough, you had to build in a flexibility that would be used. So much is built in the name of flexibility that is somehow never used. And that did work. The system was and is still being used.

commercially. He would have preferred a royalty, which would have removed some of the business responsibilities, but when he proposed a royalty arrangement, he was offered only one percent. "Continuing that way was going to be too ruinous to how I saw my life. I was over my head, terrified."

While he sincerely believed he had "made a connection" between what interested him and a product that was in the public good—"It was the cheapest thing going"—the commercialism rankled. One promotional brochure reads: "Whenever the line is shown it creates excitement translated into sales on the part of buyers of all ages, divergent tastes and socio-economic backgrounds."

I have this anti-commercialism about me—I work with clients and get involved with their commercial needs, but it plays against my grain when it comes to my own situation. I'm not into style; I'm against style.

The furniture came onto the market in April of 1972. "Within weeks I was published in every major newspaper in the U.S. I was fascinated with how people accepted it. I was into it; I was a star," he says. "But it was about furniture; it was bothering me." The furniture lasted until June, when Gehry stopped it. His withdrawal caused ill feelings. "Irwin got furious, he was a part owner," and it did not die easily. "It took a year to kill it. I had meetings to sell the patent, a lot of meetings. It got so painful, I was consciously avoiding being a furniture designer, and stayed away from furniture for the next few years." He adds, "But I had my ideas."

Gehry's Los Angeles friends have odd pieces from this time—still in use after fourteen years, still wearing well. You occasionally come across a chair in a living room; perhaps a cat has trimmed its claws on one edge, but it stands up to normal use and abnormal abuse remarkably well (a bit more rawness does not hurt). The strong profile lines of the furniture remain, and still carry it.

In 1974 Gehry developed the interiors for The Rouse Company Headquarters he was designing in Columbia, Maryland. As in the Magnin project, he completely cleared the ceiling of any fixtures and ducts, using columns instead for the mechanical feeds. Upturned floor lamps provided indirect lighting; fabric-covered wall panels took the place of acoustic tiles on the ceiling. The wall panel system he developed was different from the then standard office panels that divided a floor into separate cubicles. Gehry proposed low and intermediate panels, to create a more up and down landscape that would facilitate communication among people on the floor. Because of the clean ceiling and wall surfaces, the overall effect of the interior was cubic and monolithic.

"It was a critique of the state-of-the-art open landscape office, with its mechanistic wall panel system," says Gehry. "I wanted really flexible units that allowed for more individual treatment within each person's space." Gehry encouraged Rouse to use its old furniture within the landscape; he wanted people to bring in their own personal effects.

Berger, Berger, Kahn, Shafton & Moss Law   1977
Los Angeles, California

Furniture Gehry designed
for the law offices of Berger,
Berger, Kahn, Shafton &
Moss was a reaction against
the sameness of the office
landscape environment that
prevailed in the 1970s. The
slat benches and oversized
chairs were all unique, oddly
shaped pieces, upholstered
in traditional velour.

There was, then, an emphasis both on form and informality, even in the corporate headquarters of a national firm. Gehry was trying to personalize the corporate environment.

In offices finished in 1977 for the Los Angeles law firm, Berger, Berger, Kahn, Shafton & Moss, Gehry abandoned a systems approach to office design in favor of a more episodic landscape built of wood-stud walls and Sheetrock—the oddly angled, partial walls and the irregularly placed light troughs created a high-energy environment with no modular repetition. In it Gehry designed one-of-a-kind pieces of furniture, of exaggerated size and odd proportions—it was an oddness for the sake of risk, and clearly a break from Easy Edges, so formally appealing with its light, whimsical, but somewhat safe forms. The lawyers' reception of the furniture was mixed, and two armchairs they rejected now furnish Gehry's office. They are not particularly comfortable; the eye does not linger on them; they are a search beyond beauty—this is furniture that is intentionally difficult and awkward. "You grow by giving yourself impossible problems," he says. There was a wide range of pieces done for the lawyers, from cardboard furniture, to lacquered pieces, to those with suede upholstery.

By the late 1970s Gehry had firmly established a national and international reputation, with his own house (1977-1978), the Cabrillo Marine Museum (1979), Santa Monica Place (1973-1980), and the Spiller House (1980), but the cardboard chair still captured his imagination and he tinkered with new transformations of the basic idea. The chairs are now a sideline, approached within the security of an established architectural practice. From 1979 through 1982 his investigation of cardboard centered on stacking sheets with the fluting parallel rather than crossed. He was also interested in larger flutes and in mixing cardboard with fluting of different sizes. The exposed surfaces result in greater irregularities, and are more prone to checking than those of Easy Edges.

I was having dinner with the architect-publisher Ricky Wurman and he asked me if we could work on something together. I said we could make furniture by the slice, like a Jewish deli—like a salami on rye, or pastrami on something. That appealed to his marketing sensibility.

The intersection of furniture by the slice and large flutes inspired the formation of Furniture Brothers (Frank and Ricky), an entity that created a line called Experimental Edges—thick chunks of large-fluted cardboard, with ruffled edges, mis-stacked on each other. The furniture seemed to be unraveling at its edges, in a state of decomposition. Some, like the armchairs, were designed in greatly exaggerated cartoon shapes, similar to the upholstered pieces for Berger, Berger. Max Protetch, the New York gallery owner, liked the furniture and sold it in his 57th Street gallery. Some of the pieces had fragments of polished marble on top. "Ricky put the marble on top—he tried to give it a haircut. But it wasn't tame."

Shortly after Experimental Edges, Bloomingdale's briefly brought back Easy Edges, though Gehry remembers that the person who fabricated it did not sand the surface, which gave the pieces an uncharacteristic hardness. Gehry continues to work on the corrugated furniture today, a full seventeen years after the first cardboard furniture created for Joseph Magnin. The new series builds on previous efforts. The fluting is very large, the edges very rough, and the overall shapes even more typological and exaggerated. Armchairs have large arms, backs are high; the corrugated pieces are stacked in strata that are at times geological. Unlike Easy Edges, with its elegantly linear profiles, these pieces are solids.

If furniture for Gehry was no longer an extension of a building, some of his buildings became, instead, large pieces of furniture. The chapel at Loyola Law School in Los Angeles, paneled in an elegantly finished and stained plywood, with detailed joinery, is, for Gehry, a piece of furniture sitting in the outdoor plaza as though it were a dresser in a room. The idea for a furniture building grew out of the Smith House, an unbuilt project in Brentwood, designed in 1981, in which the master bedroom was a semi-detached building sheathed in wood with articulated joints.

The Smith House was indirectly also the source of another of Frank Gehry's pieces of furniture—his fish lamp. Having seen so many architects use classical buildings as references in their work, Gehry decided to look instead to nature for forms. On the driveway side of the Smith House, he thought of building a colonnade—"a first line of objects, smaller in scale." (The house addition was broken down into its constituent rooms, each expressed as a small separate building "object.") But, he says, the columns became a row of animals. The first was to be an eagle (as in the Chicago Tribune Tower project, p 126) built in concrete and glass. "Then I started designing fish, standing up. I became fascinated with the perfection and variety of their forms."

The first public unveiling of the fish as a formal interest of Gehry, however, was in The New York Architectural League's *Collaboration* exhibition held in 1981, in which architects and artists were invited to collaborate on a single project. Gehry teamed with sculptor Richard Serra to create a suspension bridge: on one end the suspension bridge is held up by an abstract Serra pylon; at the other end is a 150-story Gehry fish leaning backwards in the water. Gehry designed a mock-up of fish scales in glass, having gone to artist Dewain Valentine, who worked with glass, for advice. "The first time I saw the real potential of it [the fish] was when I made the model of the scales of glass for the bridge project. I loved the look of that layering of the glass. I don't know that I really want to build a fish building."

Inspired by a coiled snake proposed by Serra for a Los Angeles project, Gehry added the snake to his bestiary and displayed both the snake and the fish in the exhibition of follies held at the Castelli Gallery in New York in 1983: the snake was to be a prison conveniently located on the grassy estate of a wealthy person who had everything; the glass fish was a pavilion. "Once you start thinking about scales, there's an obvious continuity. You can do armadillos. Now I'm doing crocodiles." In Rebecca's restaurant, the architect has designed large ceiling-mounted crocodiles that serve as overhead lights. There is also an octopus chandelier, as well as two glass fish lamps.

The first fish lamps were created as a result of the promotional use of the new Colorcore. Gehry, along with many other architects, was asked by the Formica Corporation to use the new, uniformly colored plastic laminate in an inventive way. "I did my usual research with the material, analyzing what it could do. I found that the warm colors were translucent, and the colder ones, opaque." He tried to make some lamps out of the warm colors, but Gehry says they looked like frozen Noguchi lamps. "I could bend and warp it, but it was so rigid. I got angry one day and broke the material. I looked down at the floor and there were all these beautiful little flints. I said, 'Tomasz, make a fish.'" The fish that the Polish artist working for the firm made is the one now in Gehry's house. People started asking for them and, like the Experimental Edges, they found their way into galleries. With the fish, Gehry reversed his usual process of transforming a cheap material: here he transformed one of the most finished of commercial materials into one with raw-ness—Colorcore is perhaps the quintessential veneer, and he broke it up, or deconstructed it. Irregular fragments were the basic building blocks, the chips became the scales; larger fragments composed the base. The light still glows through the translucent material but the edges are now rough. About thirty, all different, were produced by New City Editions, Venice, California, in association with Frank Gehry, and first exhibited at the Larry Gagosian Gallery in Los Angeles and subsequently in New York at Metro Pictures. Although the lamps may issue some light, they hardly qualify as usable lamps. They are works of art first and only minimally lamps.

Prone to holding onto and slightly changing the same idea many times, Gehry is also able to transform the same idea at many scales. He planned at one time to cover a chair in Formica fish scales, and he proposed fish scales for the roof of his amphitheater at the Louisiana World Exposition: "Can you imagine that roof in fish scales, glowing at night?" he asks. The dramatically sloped roof, shaped like a fan, with clipped wings, was originally to have translucent roofing shaped like scales, but budget cuts made the roof impracticable. It was finally covered in corrugated metal.

The fish figure has darted in and out of many studies over several years, appearing as a hotel in a sketch project for Kalamazoo in 1981, in the Loyola Law School chapel belfry, and in sketches for the Wosk Residence of 1982-1984 and the Hauserman work station of 1983. "Whenever I'd draw something and I couldn't finish the design,

The Prison, from *Follies* 1983
New York City

The project was Barbara Jakobson's funny idea. She concocted it and invited a number of people to participate at Leo Castelli's Gallery. I really wanted to do a tract house, which was her original idea, so when the folly idea came up I was caught off guard. I had been doing some work with the fish form, and though Barbara begged me not to do anything with the fish form, I couldn't see anything else. I suppose when you're on some kind of

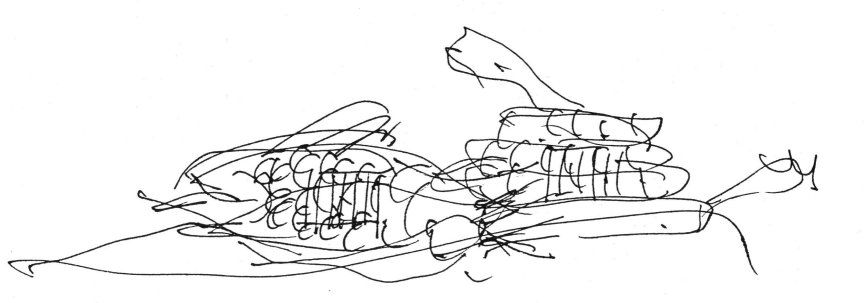

track it's hard to stop, it's hard to get off. I came up with the idea of a prison for a burglar. It was a funny idea. The design was for a wealthy landowner, in case the police didn't arrive on time. It had all kinds of double meanings—they were intuitive, I didn't contrive them—there were all kinds of options, all kinds of implications in putting somebody in prison in a snake, and wheeling people out into a fish to look at the prisoner. But I proceeded with that idea. A folly's a folly after all. The snake became part of my

entourage from a collaboration with Richard Serra, an earlier collaboration where I was doing fish buildings and Richard talked about coiled snakes. The idea fascinated me, so I placed the two disparate objects together, not unlike a lot of the work I've been doing in which disparate objects are put together. A fish and a snake are a nice contrast in form and in texture, and I tried to explore those things here. Subsequently we've built a huge fish in Italy, thirty-five feet long, for a display that is quite similar to the folly.

Sketch for *The Prison*   1983
ink on paper
8½ x 11
Collection the architect

Gehry's original sketch indicates a more aggressive snake than the one finally created for the folly exhibition's model (opposite).

I'd draw the fish as a notation." The fish figure served as an agent provocateur for some kind of built object, as yet to be designed.

During a career spanning more than thirty years, Gehry has gone from buildings with built-in furniture to furniture that is a building. He has also migrated from design informed by the notion of industrial production to design informed by notions of art. The department store commercialism has disappeared, to be replaced by that of the gallery system and the art world.

His cardboard furniture perhaps best embodies and focuses the evolution of his work, exemplifying his transition from an architect who does not design furniture to an architect who does not make art. Always an architect, or mostly an architect, he is tenacious about an idea, and playful and deliberate in his search for an oddness and rawness rich in complexity and ambiguity. The pieces that catch the eye first also sustain a long reading. They are objects that show a process of becoming, whether construction or deconstruction; and they are about the artistic exploration of materiality: you touch this furniture. In the most recent work, representational imagery has become a subject. Images of the armchair and the fish have emerged within pieces that remain strongly cardboard and Formica: there are interesting tensions between the material and the representational idea. Though the images do not act with the social symbolism of an Oldenburg, some do tap into strong, perhaps more private and archetypal associations. Gehry has said, "The coiled snake symbolizes hostility and embodies fear."

During his career, Gehry has distanced himself from the design caution that large commercial commissions and marketing restrictions at first imposed. If he is now the architectural member in good standing of the art world, it is not only because the work draws on artistic methods with artistic results, but also because the approval, interest and protection of the art world give him encouragement and allow him great freedom. Gehry has found a clientele for his imagination—one already predisposed to "edge" and "difficult work" rather than convention and conservatism. In this context he can progress from project to project in the inventive increments that typify his growth and make each new project so unexpected.

Low White Fish Lamp   1984
Colorcore, wire, wood,
incandescent lights
38 x 63 47
Courtesy New City Editions

(lower left)
Basket Snake   1984
Colorcore, wire, wood,
incandescent lights
34 x 48 x 26
©Frank Gehry/
New City Editions
Venice, California

(lower right)
Pesce Grande   1986
plywood, metal, glass
120 x 444 x 144
Produced by and collection
Gruppo Finanziario Tessile
Frank Gehry design in
association with
New City Editions,
Venice, California

Spiller House 1980
Venice, California

The Spiller House is actually two houses—a two-story rental unit on the street side, and a four-story house for its owner in the rear. Here Gehry uses the same corrugated metal siding on the exterior that forms the second skin around his own house.

Coming off of the work on my house, the Spiller House utilized rough framing and probably came closer to the intent of the unbuilt Familian House than anything else I'd done. The interior feels very trellislike; you're in a cage with rough wood framing. It was also the beginning of the two objects placed one against the other in a tight site, similar to de Menil and later becoming Benson.

The other idea I played with here was to put up a frame with no windows, no headers or cutouts for windows, with the idea that I would go up there and place the windows, just nail them on and build around them. The strange thing was that I found that the windows, as we'd designed them, as we'd conceived of the house, were perfect. So we left the windows the way they were on the

In the Spiller living room a light well cuts through the tall vertical space, creating patterns on the walls with the shadows of the wood framework.

Sketch for Spiller
House   1980
ink on paper
11 x 8½
Collection the architect

Gehry's early sketch roughly describes the roofscape that as built includes solar panels, the wood and glass frames of the skylights, trellises and stairs.

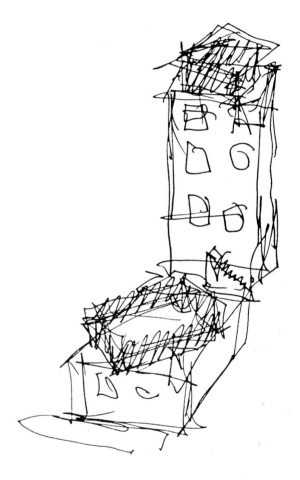

model. As it turned out, there was no advantage to this system except for the nice quality of the framework going through, which in that site gave a layer of privacy to the interior.

In this house the owner was obsessed with detail. She acted as owner-builder with a small construction firm. Consequently she was able to handpick all the lumber, so that the rough carpentry became very refined. It was interesting to see the carpenters being very craftsmanlike with the joinery of the rough framing.

Santa Monica Place   1973-1980
Santa Monica, California

Approaching Santa Monica Place by car from the south is an extraordinary experience; its name, in blue and white veils of chain link, provides a unique, indelible graphic image that can be read at any speed.

By the end of this project I realized the limits of my interest in trying to please the marketplace. The whole process became a conflict between my architectural interests and the client's perception of the American buying public's sense of place, sense of needs, sense of a comfortable place to shop. So I

don't look on Santa Monica Place as a completed work that I go back to, although I'm very interested in the problem and the typology. The direction shopping malls have taken toward placating the public or second guessing the public, of in effect talking down to the public, I find very disturbing. To think

The interior of the shopping mall focuses on a large skylit core that is surrounded by light-filled passageways and shops. Because of the variety of spatial experiences and the architect's sensitivity to the need for light and air, Santa Monica Place is set apart from other urban malls of its period.

of making these fantasy spaces, that are unconnected to reality, permanent public space, bothers me. I love fantasy in movies, I love it in art, but when the fantasy starts to manipulate your feelings, and encourages you to do things that you might not want to do, like shop, I am concerned.

All of what I've just said represents very personal feelings, and in no way is intended to be critical of what goes on, because Lord knows a lot of people do like it. I'm hoping a developer will come along who wants to deal with this kind of shopping phenomenon in a new way, to solve a problem at a higher level.

Mildred Friedman

Fast Food

The reason I do furniture and lamps and exhibitions is because it's like fast food. It's quick nourishment . . . it moves, it's built, it's done. It's very exciting. It's theatrical.[1]

Layers of chain-link fencing created a mysterious scrimlike veil behind the double stage designed by Gehry for *Available Light,* Lucinda Childs's 1983 inaugural dance work for Los Angeles's Temporary Contemporary museum.

Frank Gehry's close friendships with many painters and sculptors, and his unabashed admiration of their work have led some observers to suggest that, at heart, he regards himself more as artist than architect. But he denies this, and proves the point with his buildings, which are totally expressive of architectural considerations. His intense involvement with space, structure and light and with the practical and psychological needs of his clients are the concerns of pure architecture. Yet, analogies with painting and sculpture persist in his work.

Gehry searches for ways to give his buildings the appearance of being "in-process." In the late 1970s, such characteristic elements as exposed studs and unpainted walls allowed the architect to explore fully the inherent nature of materials and express their qualities in unexpected relationships. Since the early 1980s, he has often disassembled projects—particularly his houses—into small, one-room units that he then groups into villagelike clusters. "A one-room building," he maintains, "forces one to think about the basic issues of space. This is as close as I can get to the place of a painter facing a white canvas."

In contrast to many of his colleagues, Gehry does not make overt references to history, except, of course, in the post, beam, column essentials of an architectural vocabulary. Instead, his unique use of materials and his formal vocabulary are fueled by an intense desire to invent new forms, and in so doing he "looks for awkward connections— like a jazz player just off the note." To achieve this end he often uses what are generally construed to be painterly devices such as distorted perspective and a cubistic layering of space.

These attitudes and methods feed into Gehry's activities that, in various degrees, fall outside the realm of his architectural practice. Though it is not unusual for an architect to design furniture and lamps, Gehry's extensive experience with installation design for exhibitions

1. Unless otherwise noted, the architect's comments are excerpts from interviews with the author conducted on various occasions in 1984 and 1985.

Art Treasures of Japan 1965
**Los Angeles County Museum of Art,
California**

These views of the
installation for *Art Treasures
of Japan* indicate the
simplicity and elegance of
the surroundings Gehry
provided for the exhibition's
extraordinary ancient
objects. Wood framing, river
pebbles and red silk panels
define warm backgrounds
appropriate to the scale and
materials of the works of art.

2. Greg Walsh made a tape for the author in 1985, in
which he describes the exhibition designs that have
been undertaken by the Gehry office since 1965.

of historical and contemporary art and, more recently, his adventures
in the design of settings for performance art distinguish his practice.
Gehry is fatally attracted to the other visual arts and to the artists who
create them. They provide an element in his diet from which he apparently acquires essential intellectual nourishment.

Yet, it was not Gehry's friendships with artists that led to his first
commission to design an exhibition installation at the Los Angeles
County Museum of Art—a relationship with that institution that has
been ongoing, on a project basis, since 1965. It began through Gehry's
longtime friend and associate Greg Walsh, who was his classmate at
U.S.C.'s School of Architecture and who has been in practice with Gehry
since the early 1960s. Walsh's knowledge of Japanese art led the
museum to him and to the Gehry office for assistance in the design of
a complex exhibition: *Art Treasures of Japan.*[2] Gehry and Walsh collaborated on this initial effort for the museum, as they have on a number
of subsequent projects. Perhaps because it was their first major exhibition design, it was undoubtedly their most conservative and
"museumlike" in conception and execution.

The space in which most of the Los Angeles County's temporary
exhibitions were housed, before the recent building additions, was a
difficult one: a long, narrow space with fifteen-foot-high ceilings with
a gridwork of light tracks and acoustical tile more appropriate to an
office than to a museum, and what Walsh describes as odd "bumps"
on the two long walls.

In their approach to exhibition design, Walsh says three basic elements come into play: the curatorial view of the work to be shown;
Gehry's personal response to the material; and, the obligation to provide information for the viewer. For the Japanese exhibition, the central
problem was to evoke the original settings of the ancient works without
literally re-creating them. One approach was through the use of
Japanese room scale. The architects lowered the perceived height of
the gallery by adding a wood band around the top of the partitions
that were only ten feet high. By treating raised platforms as floors, they
allowed a standing observer to see objects as they might be seen from
a seated position. For in old, and often in new, Japan domestic activities
are associated with a "floor culture." In addition to adjusting the visitor's
point of view, the raised platforms, sometimes covered with areas of
raked sand or smooth pebbles, provided protection for the largest objects, keeping the viewer at a reasonable distance. Panels of red silk
were stretched on poles below the ceiling light grid to create diffused
light and to eliminate from view the ever-present, intrusive fixtures.

Through such artifice, the character of the gallery was quite literally
Japanized, but it was Japan with overtones of Frank Lloyd Wright that
flowed naturally from Gehry's architecture of that time. Gehry's early
work had been strongly influenced by Wright and though the decorative
aspects of Wright's architecture have been eliminated from Gehry's

built work, he has retained the asymmetrical plan and abiding concern with materials that are hallmarks of the Wrightian style.

Over the years Gehry's museum installations have consistently contained ideas that were emerging simultaneously in his architecture. His next project for the County Museum, *Billy Al Bengston,* in 1968, is a primary example of this tendency. A close friend of the artist who had requested that he design the exhibition, Gehry took on the assignment with gusto. He created an environment in the gallery that reflected the artist's "L.A. Biker" persona. At that time Bengston used auto-metallic paints to create shimmering patterns of stars and stripes derived from motorcycle lore. Gehry, in attempting literally to re-create the artist's studio in the museum, went so far as to bring Bengston's studio furniture into the gallery—lamps, chairs, books and all. And for the first time, Gehry used unpainted corrugated metal, unpainted plywood and exposed wood studs. Views through the open stud walls allowed a sense of what had not yet been seen, a Gehryism that occurs again and again in many of his buildings and exhibition designs.

Bengston's glowing metallic heraldry was presented as it might have been encountered in its natural habitat. The museum staff actively disliked the installation, but the artist and the audience loved it. The exhibition looked undesigned, but Walsh asserts this was only apparent casualness, another persistent characteristic of Gehry's work.

In 1980 Gehry was given what he regards as the ultimate opportunity in exhibition design, the County Museum's *The Avant-Garde in Russia, 1910-1930: New Perspectives.* The exhibition, comprised of over five hundred paintings, sculptures, graphics, architectural models, costumes and theatrical set designs, chronicled twenty years of Russian constructivist art. Although all of the material was borrowed from collections in the West, the bulk of it was almost entirely unknown in the United States. Working with curator Stephanie Barron, Gehry and Greg Walsh developed a scenario for this extraordinarily complex material on a large wall in their office. After several meetings in which pieces of paper representing the objects were moved around the wall in an effort to develop coherent groupings, a structure began to emerge. Twelve distinct sections were decided upon, and a route through the exhibition was determined.

As had been true in the Japanese exhibition, many of the Russian paintings, graphics, books and models were relatively small. In order to scale-down the galleries, Gehry made the walls only ten feet high, but he carried their framework to the ceiling, once again creating an open-stud system of unpainted wood, consistent with the spirit of the Russian material. The Sheetrock-covered walls were painted red, white and black; sculpture bases and cases for books and printed ephemera were unpainted plywood. Vintage photographs, collected by Stephanie Barron, provided clues to the informal way the Russians had installed works in exhibitions of the period. Gehry paced the exhibition with

The first appearance in Gehry's work of corrugated metal siding occurred in his design for the Los Angeles County Museum's 1968 exhibition of paintings by Billy Al Bengston. Used here to evoke the artist's own studio environment, this material is seen often in the architect's buildings well into the 1980s.

Bengston's studio
surroundings, down to the
chairs and tables, were used
by Gehry to literally re-create
the painter's milieu within
the museum.

***The Avant-Garde in Russia, 1910-1930: New Perspectives* 1980**
Los Angeles County Museum of Art, California

Cases of unfinished plywood contained books and other small-scale printed matter in the Los Angeles County Museum's 1980 exhibition of early twentieth-century Russian art. Gehry's designs for the cases and partitioning walls created a structural framework that permitted vistas from one section to another and related strongly to the character of the works being shown.

A vintage photograph of
Malevich's section of the
1915 *0-10* exhibition
provided the information for
the design of this section of
the Russian installation. An
enlargement of the original
image was included in
Gehry's reconstruction.

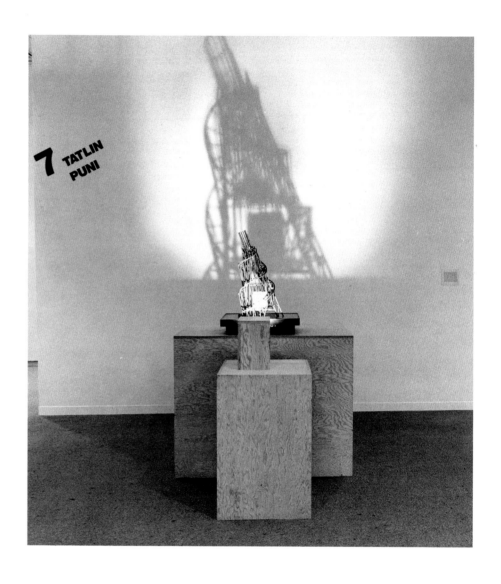

7 TATLIN PUNI

Varvara Stepanova's 1922 set for *Tarelkin's Death* was reconstructed for the 1980 exhibition by Douglas Reed and Ah Sim Lee, under the supervision of Paul Lubowicki of Frank O. Gehry and Associates.

This small-scale model of Vladimir Tatlin's proposed *Monument to the Third International,* 1920, was carefully lighted to create the illusion of the larger reality.

(opposite)
The ingenuity of Gehry's case design is seen in this view of the Russian exhibition. Throughout, framed drawings and paintings were hung above the printed matter to emphasize chronological and iconographic relationships.

Seventeen Artists in the Sixties 1981
**Los Angeles County Museum of Art,
California**

tight groupings of paintings interspersed with works in other media in an attempt to recapture the character of the places in which these avant-garde works had originally been seen and, not incidentally, to offset the museum fatigue inevitable in such a vast presentation.

Gehry felt strong "resonances" between these pioneer Russians and himself, between their searching idealism and his own experimental bent. Therefore, re-creating Varvara Stepanova's 1922 stage set for *Tarelkin's Death,* and the *0-10* installation of suprematist works by Kasimir Malevich seemed natural to Gehry, almost easy. Reasons for his choices of methods and materials were, of course, quite different from those that had motivated the Russians, whose aesthetic clearly derived in part from the need to make do, to use whatever was at hand. Their forms, to some degree, reflected their economic plight. On the other hand, Gehry's use of such unadorned, simple materials in his exhibition design came out of his sensitivity to the constructivist idiom and its relationship to his architecture. In his own Santa Monica house (1977-1978), and in the Spiller House (1980), he had used the corrugated metal (first seen in the 1968 Bengston installation) and the exposed wood framing that had been consistent elements in his work for several years. Missing in the museum installation was the spatial freedom of the houses, with their irregular fenestration, open stairways and exhilarating use of natural light—qualities that were inconsistent with the essential demands of the Russian exhibition material, as well as with the difficult space of the gallery. Despite these restrictions, the installation of the Russian exhibition was enormously successful. While the historical importance of the subject matter might have elicited a more traditional museological treatment from other hands, Gehry gave it an immediacy, a sense of surprise that is entirely appropriate to the character of the art and to the era of Russian history it represents.

In 1981, an exhibition called *Seventeen Artists in the Sixties* at the County Museum included works by many artists whom Gehry had known for over twenty years. In his installation, each artist's work was shown in a small room, individual galleries organized along a central spine. Many of the walls had large cutout openings that allowed views of the spaces beyond. In contrast to the design of the Russian exhibition, these walls were completely covered with Sheetrock, painted in soft earth tones and white to provide a neutral ground for the works.

In distinct contrast to that minimalist installation of perforated cubes was Gehry's richly variegated scheme for the County Museum's exhibition of German expressionist sculpture. Stephanie Barron, who organized this 1983 exhibition of one hundred fifty extraordinary sculptures, included many by artists who were little known in the U.S. Because so much of their work had been destroyed by the Nazis in the 1930s, and to create the atmosphere of anxiety and repression surrounding this material, Gehry suggested the use of chain-link mesh fencing as a backdrop for the sculpture, an idea that was rejected by the museum, he says, as perhaps too powerful. Instead, because the gallery ceiling had been painted black for a previous show (and that color was retained, for economy's sake) Barron and Gehry decided to have one of the gallery's long walls painted black as a background for photographs of many of the works that had been destroyed. With these, photographs of book burnings and Nazi propaganda documents created what Greg Walsh has characterized as a "somber terminus" to the views of each section of the exhibition.

Even though chain link was ruled out, Gehry used a wide array of materials in this installation: natural-finish stucco, brick, raw plywood, the dark Finnish plywood of the Loyola Law School chapel, painted wood, polished hardwood and metallic auto paints. Colors were dark and grayed-back. However, the large-scale photographs, used to illustrate the destroyed works, in some cases overwhelmed the small sculptures next to them, and they often diluted the impact of the objects. In the end, the complexly carved, often painted wood sculptures might have been better seen against the chain link of Gehry's original proposal. Given the nature of this narrative sculpture, with its extensive religious and social "baggage," the curator and Gehry may have attempted to say more than can be encompassed by an installation environment.

In exhibition design, the works of art become the client and the designer provides an environment in the service of art. Because of his associations with artists, it was inevitable that Gehry would move from the design of exhibitions to collaboration with artists in the creation of works that metaphorically bridge the gap between art and architecture. His initial joint effort with the sculptor Richard Serra was coincidentally the design of a bridge for the exhibition *Collaboration: Artists & Architects* (1981). Serra had made an extraordinary film in 1976— *Railroad Turnbridge*—which Gehry greatly admired, and though neither had ever designed a bridge, both men were attracted to the idea. From the windows of Serra's New York loft, they looked out on the World Trade Center on one side and the Chrysler Building on the other. For their collaboration, they decided to join them with an elaborately conceived bridge. They began by making a series of huge, eight-foot-high drawings, finally arriving at a preliminary design some days later. After consultation with Skillings Engineers, they realized the need for stabilizing elements that could bear the structural load of such a long span. Two anchoring pylons were visualized: Gehry drew a huge fish that seems to be jumping out of the Hudson River just beyond the World Trade Center; Serra created a tilted pylon in the East River near the Chrysler Building. These two elements were to hold the cables in the tension necessary to support the proposed monumental bridge. This visionary project was the first public appearance of what has since become Gehry's ubiquitous fish. (See the "fish story" in Hines, page 13.)

In the same year as the Serra collaboration, Gehry drew a colonnade across the facade of the Smith House, in which each column represented

(opposite)
The Los Angeles County Museum organized an exhibition in 1981 celebrating the 1960s work of seventeen Los Angeles artists. In Gehry's design for the installation, individual rooms were created for each artist. The walls were punctuated with rectangular openings permitting views beyond each space to the next.

German Expressionist Sculpture 1983
Los Angeles County Museum of Art, California

This exhibition of 150
German expressionist
sculptures, photographs
and graphics made between
1900 and the early 1930s
included works by Ernst
Ludwig Kirchner (top),
shown with photographs of
sculptures destroyed in the
Nazi era.

A major focus of the
exhibition was a
reconstruction of a brick
church facade in which an
Ernst Barlach sculpture was
placed in a niche,
approximately as it might
have been seen in situ.

Three life-size wood figures
were placed in a plexi-
glass-walled room on a
wood floor. The separation
of sculpture and viewer was
minimized and an illusion of
shared space created by the
frameless transparent wall
on one side of the room.

Gehry-Serra Bridge for *Collaboration: Artists & Architects* 1981

Installation view of the Frank Gehry-Richard Serra bridge design for the exhibition *Collaboration: Artists & Architects* organized by The Architectural League of New York in 1981.

Sketch for *Collaboration* 1981
ink on paper
8⅛ x 10¾
Collection the architect

Gehry and Serra conceived a connection between the World Trade Center and the Chrysler Building, with anchoring elements in the East and Hudson Rivers.

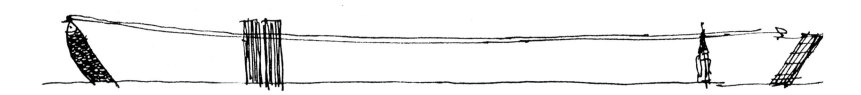

The Chrysler Building was
drawn punctured by two sets
of cables that would connect
Gehry's fish and Serra's
pylon.

3. Ironically, Gehry has often used this vernacular
architectural type in project models, but it rarely
survives into the building stage.

a different bird or fish. This proposed remodeling of a house Gehry
had designed in 1959 was never carried out, but the project became
the testing ground for a variety of ideas that continue to appear as
elements in his formal vocabulary. Outside of the recent lamps (described by Joseph Giovannini), the fish has been realized recently in
Florence, Italy on a grand scale. Constructed of plywood and glass this
thirty-six-foot long giant fish out of water is used as a prop for a fashion
show. Twelve feet wide and eight feet high it seems capable of swallow-
ing people, in the manner of Jonah's whale.

Always interested in untried methods and the invention of new
forms, Gehry has long admired the work of the sculptor Claes
Oldenburg, and he was eager to have an Oldenburg sculpture on the
Loyola Law School campus. Their cooperation in the realization of that
project led to an active collaboration between Gehry, Oldenburg and
Oldenburg's wife, the art historian and critic Coosje van Bruggen. (See
her description of their collaboration, page 128.) Gehry recalls how
they got started on what turned out to be a major statement for all
three—Camp Good Times (1984-1985). Los Angeles acquaintances of
Gehry's who were involved in an effort to build a camp for terminally
ill children, primarily cancer victims, had come to him for the planning
and design of the proposed facility, to be located in the Santa Monica
Mountains. Gehry discussed the camp with the Oldenburgs and invited
them to work on it with him. As devoted parents, both Gehry and the
Oldenburgs were drawn to this project and all three approached it
enthusiastically. As Gehry remembers it: "The Oldenburgs came to my
office daily for two weeks. They just sat there and watched me work,
watched what an architect does. Claes made models of his own. The
question of whether the camp would be architecture or art never was
asked. We wanted to blur the lines," Gehry recalls.

Out of several such sessions, over a six-month period, poured a
torrent of daringly inventive imagery that challenges the limits of both
art and architecture. The collaboration was a genuine team effort.
Oldenburg's sculpture became architectural and Gehry's architecture
became even more radically sculptural than it had ever been. This
synthesis resulted in a melange that can best be described as "narrative," a term loosely applied to architectural works whose forms and
references are outside traditional architecture. (See pages 134-143.)

The buildings that Gehry and the Oldenburgs proposed for the
camp are filled with familiar, descriptive forms. Some resemble boats,
one a milk can; several have wavelike roof elements that cascade over
hillsides. A manmade lake with a perimeter in the shape of the pieces
of a jigsaw puzzle is a landscape element in the same vein as the
buildings. A model of this plan exists, but tragically, the camp does
not. The Gehry-Oldenburg scheme was rejected and the project's fun-
ders opted for traditional log cabins.[3] What could have been a creative
landmark seems headed for architectural obscurity.

Available Light 1983
The Temporary Contemporary
The Museum of Contemporary Art
Los Angeles, California

The Museum of Contemporary Art had decided to commission performances that would bring various disciplines together. In the first program, called *Available Light*, I was put together with dancer-choreographer Lucinda Childs and John Adams, the composer. The schedule made it necessary to complete the construction of the temporary museum and open with *Available Light*. It was the first project in the space, the inaugural project. I had not worked on anything like this before, and spent a good deal of time talking to Lucinda Childs mainly, because the John Adams piece had already been written. So it was after the fact in terms of collaboration. I did spend a lot of time with Lucinda trying to figure out some way of dealing with the space and the dance so that it was a collaboration, not the Merce Cunningham tradition in which each artist goes away and does his thing and then they bring it together at the last minute. I was going back to the tradition of ballet and dancing, in which design and the music all work together to create something. That's my interest. I'd had a small encounter with Trisha Brown earlier, which never worked out. She was more inclined to work in the Cunningham tradition, and probably that's why my collaboration with her didn't work, because we never got to spend time together and really work on it.

4. From Lucinda Childs's letter to the author, 1 March 1985.

An entirely different kind of collaboration was the 1983 performance piece *Available Light,* a cooperative venture between Gehry, the dancer-choreographer Lucinda Childs and the composer John Adams. This event took place in the newly established Temporary Contemporary Museum, a spectacular warehouse space in Los Angeles's Little Tokyo district, which Gehry modified as an exhibition facility for the Los Angeles Museum of Contemporary Art. This enormous building was to be used for exhibitions while the museum's new Bunker Hill building, designed by Arata Isozaki, was under construction. As it turns out, the temporary space has been so successful in its raw, almost original state (a case of the architect knowing what to leave alone), it will be retained as exhibition space even after the new, more formal building is in use.

According to its director, Richard Koshalek, the new museum intends to sponsor a series of mixed-media collaborations, of which *Available Light* was the first. Describing Gehry's design for the dance, Lucinda Childs wrote:

He did not adorn the performance area, rather he reshaped it. This also happened in a Sol LeWitt collaboration of 1979. Both men provided a visual construct that allowed me to develop further a fundamental idea in my choreography: doubling.

LeWitt achieved this with a film of dancers projected onto a scrim above live dancers whose movements were synchronized with those in the film. The audience saw both sets at once. Gehry achieved this same effect with a split-level set. He used two freestanding wood structures, one below and in front of the other. Dancers rotated, and in the course of the fifty-minute work, all eleven danced on both levels.[4]

The vast, empty warehouse interior suggested a large performance structure, and Gehry accommodated with a double stage, forty feet wide. Its lower section was thirty-six feet deep and the rear, higher platform eighteen feet deep. A scrim of Gehry's by now iconographic chain-link fencing was hung on one side of the stage to dematerialize the space beyond. The audience was located in front and to one side of the stage. Gehry had hoped the choreography would take the two views into account, but Childs's approach was essentially frontal, in order to simplify the later transfer of the dance to the Brooklyn Academy of Music. Gehry used the building's skylight, its source of "available light," for the location of artificial light which he beamed into the space through layers of red gel. Working with the lighting designer Beverly Emmons, Gehry used this "red light" in combination with temporary theatrical lighting installed on a grid hung from the ceiling.

Dancers came and went on three stairways visible to the spectators in the open expanse of the warehouse space, and Childs incorporated this movement into her choreography. For the performance several months later at the Brooklyn Academy, Gehry created four tunnels under the overhanging upper stage platform. Through these, dancers magically appeared and disappeared. Discussing his collaboration with

I tried to give the performance the range of the space because I knew that it was unusual to have a performance in this kind of space. I was interested in inaugurating the building so that the patrons of the museum would have a sense of how big it is. I tried to use the space in a giant sense by putting a big scrim of chain link behind the dancers. We were fortunate that because of the construction schedule we were able to use the chain link that we were going to use outside on the canopy inside, so we didn't have to buy it twice. And then we put a red gel against a clerestory window way off in the distance, and that was like a sunrise or sunset which the dance played against. I was able to work with Beverly Emmons to light the building so that it would unfold spatially—all the parts of the building—so it wasn't just a stage. And then I became interested in the spectator and how the piece would be seen. I played it in two directions. The first was as a proscenium piece in which the dancers were frontal to the seating area; a second seating area was created to the side of the stage so that people seated there became spectators to a broader performance that included other spectators. The way it was lit and the way the sets were designed made the space and the performance feel larger than they were.

The double platform designed by Gehry provided spatial variation for dancers and audience. The performance was seen from two seating areas, at the front and to one side of the stage at the Temporary Contemporary. When the work was later taken to the Brooklyn Academy of Music, Gehry redesigned the set to accommodate its proscenium stage.

(below)
Available Light performance with Lucinda Childs in a Ronaldus Shamask costume. The red-gelled clerestory window creates a brilliant distant view of the space far beyond the layers of chain link fence.

Available Light

Sketches for Available Light 1983
ink on paper
11 x 14
Collection the architect

Gehry's lively early sketches indicate a broad range of possible stage forms for *Available Light*.

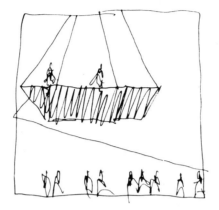

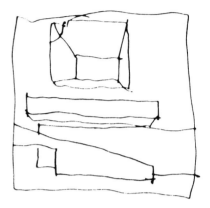

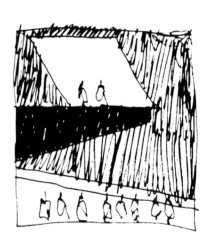

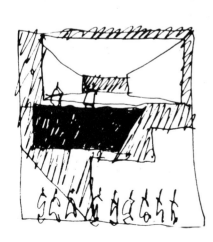

Hollywood Bowl 1970-1982
Hollywood, California

The Hollywood Bowl shell in its three configurations: (from top) the original 1929 nested quarter spheres; a 1969 interim solution using Sonotubes; and, the present system that combines the original shell with fiberglass spheres and a lighting platform hung within the shell.

5. From Julie Lazar, "Interview: Frank Gehry," *Available Light* (Los Angeles: The Museum of Contemporary Art, 1983), p 38.
6. From a telephone conversation between Ernest Fleischmann and the author, September 1985.

Childs and Adams, Gehry later recalled:

We wanted to make something that none of us would have done alone. That is the essence of collaboration. When you agree to collaborate, you agree to jump off a cliff holding hands with everyone, hoping the resourcefulness of each will insure that you all land on your feet.[5]

Gehry's experience with Childs's dance was not his first foray into the performing arts. Since 1970 he has been a consultant to the Hollywood Bowl—a natural amphitheater in the Hollywood Hills used for summer concerts. The longtime Executive Director of the Los Angeles Philharmonic Association and of the Hollywood Bowl, Ernest Fleischmann, asked him to do something about the increasingly poor acoustics of this Hollywood landmark, a favorite of southern California music lovers since its 1929 inauguration. By the time Gehry came on the scene, seating had extended beyond the original bowl shape and outside traffic had increased. The natural acoustics, augmented by the orchestra shell—a series of nested quarter spheres—were increasingly unsatisfactory.[6] Gehry, working with acoustician Christopher Jaffe, decided to supplement the existing shell with cardboard Sonotubes, a temporary solution that was employed with seasonal replacements, until 1980. A more permanent system, realized in collaboration with the Israeli acoustician Abe Melzer, is still in place. It consists of a series of fiberglass spheres hung within the shell to distribute sound to the members of the orchestra and to the audience. This solution is very satisfactory. Gehry has developed a third design, a master plan for the Bowl that would preserve the existing shell and entails building a new proscenium around it to make more elaborate staging possible.

Gehry was given an opportunity to test the feasibility of certain aspects of this plan during the 1984 Olympic Games. In celebration of the Games, a Bowl event, *Olympic Gala,* was staged by Gehry, Ron Hays, who designs laser and video animations, and the artist Peter Alexander. Gehry had wanted special NASA spotlights that have an extraordinary thirty foot beam, but they were not feasible on the Bowl's modest budget (it is a county facility). He had to settle for sixty standard, worn-out, Hollywood-extravaganza searchlights.

This celebratory visual presentation was to accompany Michael Tilson Thomas conducting Aaron Copland's *Third Symphony.* "I wanted to do Turner's skies," says Gehry, remembering the evening. "I thought I could get the fireworks going and create a light environment that would be like the paintings. I didn't want it to be boom, boom, boom—which is what the Bowl wanted and what Thomas wanted. 'When you say boom, that is when I want to shut up,' I told them."

Gehry wanted to widen the proscenium, an aspect of his third design for the shell, and this was his chance to attempt it in a temporary way with light. He and his cohorts located a very precise Swiss optical machine that is used to project color transparencies onto the Alps. They then hired a Swiss projection crew and brought it and the equipment

In celebration of the 1984 Olympic Games, Gehry, in collaboration with Ron Hays and the artist Peter Alexander, staged an event at the Hollywood Bowl. On a temporary seventy foot wide scrim, images of Turneresque painted skies were projected to accompany a performance of Aaron Copland's *Third Symphony*.

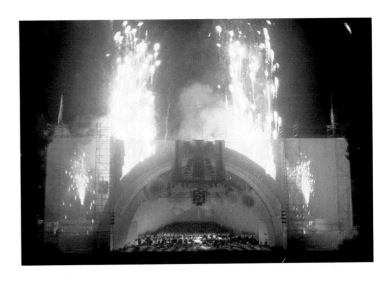
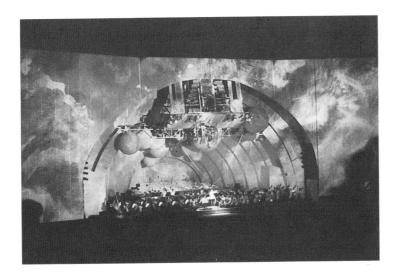

The Hollywood Bowl came to us after the Executive Director of the Hollywood Bowl, Ernest Fleischmann, had heard a concert at the Merriweather Post Pavilion in Maryland, and asked to meet the architect. Actually the involvement with the Merriweather Post Pavilion sort of whet my appetite for doing things related to the theater and to music.

When Ernest first called me it was clear they didn't have much money and that he really wanted to make an impact on the Bowl as cheaply and quickly as possible. We came up with the idea of the cardboard tubes after a meeting in which they described the acoustical problems and the focusing effect of the original shell. The cardboard Sonotubes

Hollywood Bowl

were priced out; they were very inexpensive and were intended to be up for only one season. As it turns out they stayed for about nine.

We were hired to redo the shell as part of the master plan, but the first problem to solve was the creation of a temporary shell, and then to work on the larger project. The final proposed scheme for the Bowl was to eliminate the real problem, which is the rainbow shell. It is acoustically irrelevant at this time. An outdoor structure is needed that would have all the new electronic machinery, and would not be an enclosure. We were trying to create a giant erector set or crane that could be changeable, to allow the Bowl to be more flexible for opera and other kinds of productions they now can't do. So it became kind of a mechano set, a giant technological wonder that would contain all the needed technology, essentially all exposed. We made it larger than the existing shell, which may have worked when it was grass seating years ago, but now with all the rows and rows of seating it's overpowered. Recently we did mock up that kind of thing for them for the opening of the Olympics at the Hollywood Bowl. We put up a scrim that simulated the proposed larger structure and projected huge landscape images on it.

to Los Angeles. Extending the shell's opening with a stretched scrim was not difficult; Gehry made it seventy feet high and two hundred feet wide. The question of what to project, however, was still to be resolved. Above all, Gehry did not want the performance to become a lugubrious slide lecture. He began looking for pictures of Turneresque skies, and remembered that Peter Alexander, whose studio is right down the street from his Venice office, had recently been painting a series of sky canvases. Alexander agreed to play along with Gehry's idea. Using slides of Alexander's paintings, they filled the space with light and color, and, with Michael Tilson Thomas, achieved the first genuine Hollywood son et lumière. Thus, Gehry and friends created a performance piece of a new order in the familiar surroundings of the Hollywood Bowl, replete with ravishing skies. Miraculously and entirely by coincidence, the crew of the Goodyear blimp, seeing the event in the distance, flew right into the Bowl, just in time to punctuate the finale of the performance.

Gehry rushes in where most architects fear to tread: into places like museums and theaters to create things that are generally temporary (anathema to most architects) and that must be produced in a relatively short span of time on modest budgets. Yet for Gehry, such activities are enriching, stimulating, and on occasion inspiring. These extra-architectural projects expand his horizons, taking in the eccentric, the unresolved, the unexplained aspects of the visual world that are the substance of art and of his architecture. Examining Gehry's buildings in this light brings one closer to a genuine understanding of their meaning within the context of today's architecture.

(opposite)
Frank O. Gehry and
Associates Venice,
California office, with
Wosk Residence model in
the foreground, 1986.

**House for a Filmmaker   1981
Los Angeles, California**

Sketch for a House for
a Filmmaker   1981
ink on paper
8⅛ x 10¾
Collection the architect

Gehry's sketch (below) is
pueblolike in its
arrangement of stairs and
stepped-back forms.

Views of the model indicate
the proposed disposition of
one-room buildings on the
site of this unrealized project.

**This house for a filmmaker is being completed
by another architect, due to some
circumstances beyond our control. The
original idea came from my interest in finding
the edge of my cliff, as it were. I thought that
by minimizing the issues of function, by
creating one-room buildings, we could resolve
the most difficult problem in architecture.**

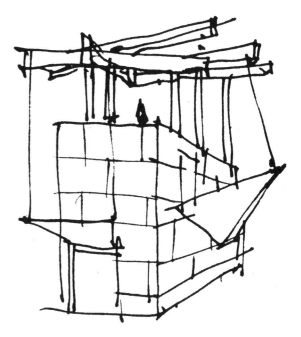

(detail)
Sketch for the House for
a Filmmaker   1981
ink on paper
10¾ x 8⅛
Collection Fred Hoffman

This sketch (which has an uncanny resemblance to the 1888 Arles painting, *The Drawbridge,* by Vincent van Gogh) shows shutters and panels that could be opened to views of a surrounding canyon.

Think of the power of one-room buildings and the fact that historically, the best buildings ever built are one-room buildings.

A filmmaker came along with an interest in engaging the outdoors, in a much more direct way than simply a house with windows. He wanted to be able to walk outside between rooms. He wasn't thinking of separate objects as much as he was thinking of the Spanish courtyard house, in which you move between the rooms and outside into a courtyard.

In this case the lot was too narrow to make a courtyard, so we ended up with long, strung out buildings, which could have been OK, too. We could have just stuck it all together and had a covered porch go the full length, like an old Spanish town. Instead, I chose to break it into separate rooms, separate objects sitting together on the site, playing off one another and exploring different materials as a way of breaking down scale. This project combined the ideas of the Davis Studio and the Jung Institute. It was my first chance to do that.

Indiana Avenue Houses   1981
Venice, California

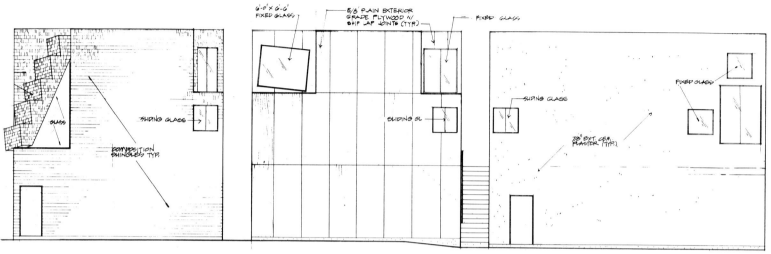

North Elevation

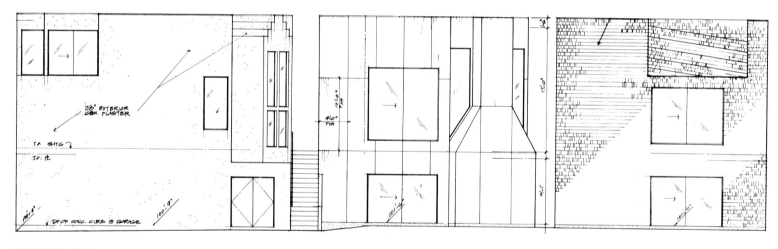

South Elevation

The Indiana Avenue Houses, designed as artists' studio-residences, are carefully composed on the small site. All of the negative spaces are significant elements in the rectangular scheme.

Chuck Arnoldi, Bill Norton and Laddie John Dill owned a lot in Venice, and they thought they could build some studios for artists and for people who wanted to hang out with artists. It was a very tight budget for three studios, but I liked the direction I was going—breaking buildings down into parts. I was also kind of angry about Postmodernism, the literal use and copying of historic details, historic elements. So I was making commentary here about stairways and fireplaces and 1930s apartment houses in

L.A. I was using those ideas as a way of humanizing a building.

Just about the time I was working on the Indiana apartments an old friend, Elaine May, and I had dinner one evening and discussed the possibility of doing a movie on architects. We spent quite a long time reinventing *Fountainhead.* But she was interested in a particular psychological problem that an architect would have who designed a building that was constructed when he was out of the country. He heard from afar that this was his

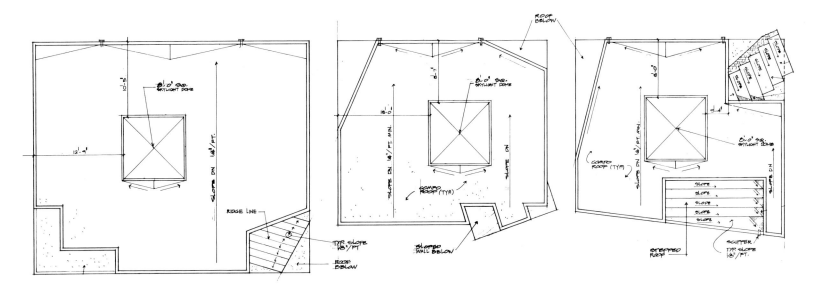

Roof Plan

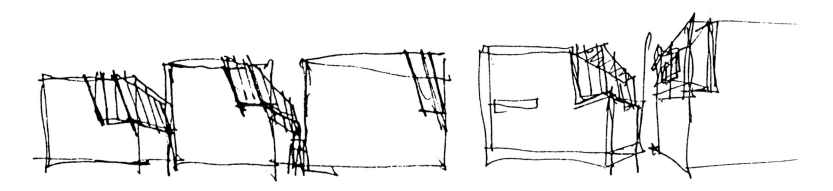

greatest work, a work of genius. The architect became incredibly famous for this building. When he returned to the U.S. and looked at the building he said, 'Oh, my God! They didn't read the plans right. There's a horrible mistake.' And it was just that mistake that made the building so exciting. The movie she wanted would start out on an analyst's couch where this poor guy was trying to deal with that issue in his life. I thought there was nothing an architect could do that would be a mistake like that. I racked my brain for ideas

for that and couldn't find any, because to make that kind of mistake would be impossible. They'd have to build a building on its side instead of vertically because the prints were printed on the side. It's not likely.

When the Indiana job came along, Chuck, Laddie and Norton took me out to see the site. We looked at the site and I got a good picture of it and of the neighborhood. I came back to the office and we built models of the site from the survey done by a certified surveyor; you can sue if they make a mistake, so they're very

(below, detail)
Sketch for Indiana Avenue
Houses   1981
ink on paper
10¾ x 8⅛
Collection the architect

Indiana Avenue Houses

Each of the three Indiana Avenue buildings is sheathed in a different material: green asphalt shingles, unpainted plywood and blue stucco, materials that seem correct in this neighborhood of small, primarily wooden bungalows.

careful. When we finished the working drawings, the job went out to bid. Just before it went out to bid I had a meeting with the artists and somebody—I forget who—said, 'Are you sure those plans are for the right site?' I thought he was a bit goofy and I didn't pay much attention. But then it occurred to me that maybe he was right, that something had happened. I was out of town, and I called Greg Walsh and said, 'Would you please check the orientation on the Indiana lot because one of the guys thought something was wrong.' So he looked at the survey and called the surveyor and it all checked out. He called me

In the interiors of the houses over-scaled windows and exposed wood structural elements create lively, sculptural forms against the bright ocean-tinted sky of Venice.

back and said 'We're right on the money. Everything's perfect.' So construction started. A few weeks later, on my way to the airport I drove by the construction with some men from the office. The foundations were already in their frames. They said, 'This is the wrong site! It's that site over there—it's across the road.' The artists had shown me the wrong site. We went back to the survey and found that the surveyor had put on the wrong north arrow, making the site drawing jive with my vision of the site. Greg had checked it out. Everything checked, except it was the site across the road. So now the building was under construction and, in a way, Elaine May's scenario happened. All the windows face south that were supposed to face north. The space we like best is wrong.

Kalamazoo Charette 1981
Kalamazoo, Michigan

Four architects were invited to Kalamazoo, Michigan for a charette: Stanley Tigerman, Robert Stern, Merrill Elam and me. We were given space in a hotel room, and each of us was given ten students from schools in the area. I could only stay three of the five days, so Greg Walsh came and spent the full time so that he could supervise.

The problem was how to put housing back into downtown Kalamazoo. The amount of housing the market showed could be brought in was very minimal—300 units. As we walked around town I found an industrial area that was very dilapidated, unused and almost abandoned. It had an underground water course, a source that emptied into the nearby river, so I decided to dam that and make a kind of lagoon, tear down all the industrial buildings, make a causeway crossing the lagoon for the main entry into town and then build a parking garage on one side of the lagoon that backs up against the historical

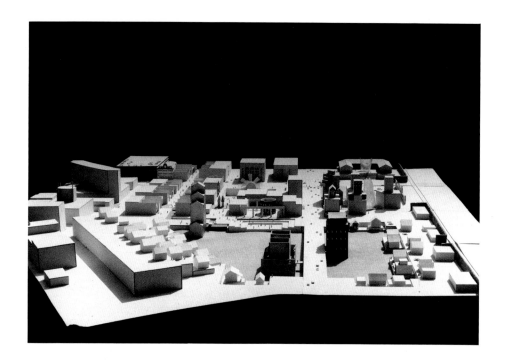

Sketch for Kalamazoo 1981
ink on paper
10¾ x 8⅛
Collection Berta Gehry

In this sketch Gehry has drawn a hotel in the shape of a fish as one of several means of achieving the diversity he believes essential to the creation of vital urban areas.

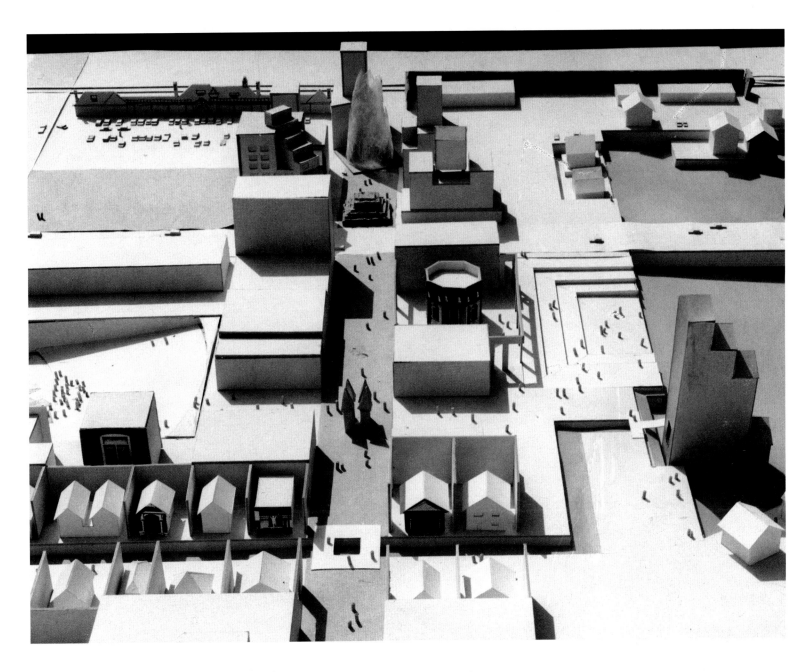

neighborhood. The parking lot would become a stair-step amphitheater on which to place houses. I proposed that the houses would be the small vernacular clapboard style of the region, which are some of the prettiest buildings in that area. In this way they became sculptures in an amphitheater of houses looking over the lagoon. As a terminus to the old Victor Gruen mall, which by the way I had worked on years ago when I was at Gruen, I proposed a hotel in the shape of a fish.

Theoretically somebody was supposed to win this competition and be selected for the job. In reality the job went to Skidmore, Owings & Merrill's Chicago office. They retained some idea of our lake but it's a more conservative scheme than the one we proposed.

A model was created for the Kalamazoo charette; in it Gehry's group made a neighborhood of small clapboard houses that look out over a proposed lagoon. A causeway, over the lagoon, provides an exciting entrance to the city.

Benson House   1981-1984
Calabasas, California

The Benson House is one of my all-time favorite projects because the budget was so tight and so impossible—tiny little lot, tiny family. Bob Benson was on the committee of Loyola that selected me for that project. Later he asked me to do his house. The idea of making two boxes started from the premise that if you could break down the scale of a building and make very simple pieces with very short spans, it would be cheaper than a single building. The richness in the project would be the differentiation of these pieces and the relationship of the different forms to each other and to the spaces they would create. The windows were placed so that when you looked out you would see corners of the building next to you and thus create your own landscape—your own environment.

(opposite)
In the Benson House model (left) a proposed treehouse-fort is shown on the roof of the brown-shingled bedroom building. On site (below), the additional roof elements are not yet completed.

On the steeply sloping site, the buildings are connected with a powerful wood stairway. Its railing defines a roof deck on the living-kitchen structure, a place to enjoy views of the surrounding hills.

I also wanted to instill it with as much fantasy as I could. I started by using the natural problems of the site, which had to be overcome. For instance, the steep bank needed a retaining wall. I could have put the house plunk against the retaining wall, but that would have created a weather proofing problem, which though solvable is, nevertheless, precarious. So I decided to make the retaining wall separate and to place

the two buildings like objects with a space between, thereby creating a moat that joined the two elements. The taller building is the bedroom building, the kids on the bottom floor and the parents upstairs. There's a secret passageway-closet-stairway that takes the kids all the way to the roof. On the roof we proposed to build a small log cabin that was a treehouse. That piece hasn't been completed.

Moatlike spaces occur between the building elements that are joined by second-story bridges (left). The kitchen has an enormous light monitor that provides views of the adjacent bedroom building and the trees and sky beyond.

Benson House

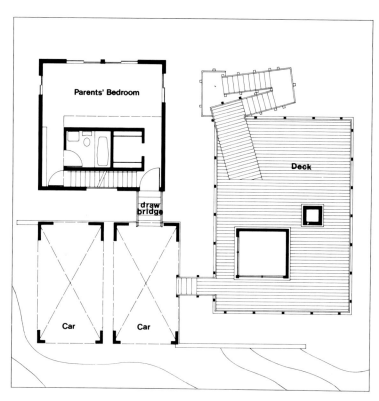

Second Floor Plan

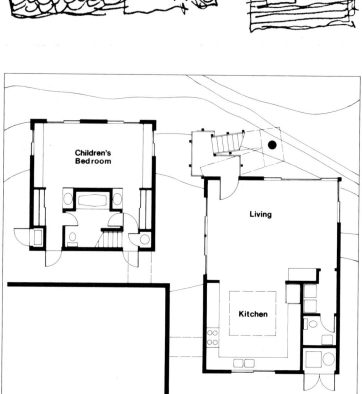

First Floor Plan

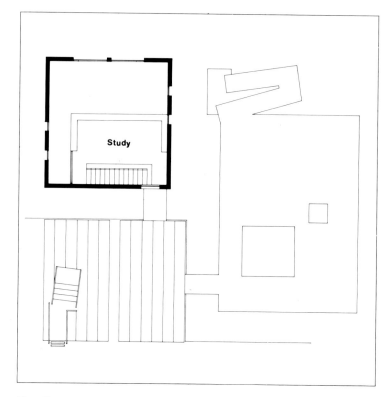

First Floor Mezzanine Plan

I wanted to have a processional entry, so from the parking area one walks up some stairs, across the roof of the living room, down some stairs into the main entrance of the living room on the view side. So then we had the rich element of a stairway in front of a large window. We used very rough carpentry; we left it exposed. On the exterior we used asphalt shingles. I'm sure that comes from looking at those little houses in Queens every time I drive in from the airport in New York. The combination of the two buildings, the skylights, the chimney, the carports, the stairways and the log cabin all creates pieces that when played against each other make these simple boxes richer.

(above and opposite)
Sketches for Benson
House   1981
10¾ x 8⅛ each
Collection the architect

Coosje van Bruggen

Leaps into the Unknown

Claes Oldenburg
*Coltello/Ship in Three
Stages* 1984
pencil, colored pencil, chalk,
watercolor
one-half of 30 x 40 sheet of
paper (with *Binoculars,*
p 130)
Collection the artist

In January 1982, while in Los Angeles, Claes Oldenburg and I visited Frank and Berta Gehry for the first time. Alejo and Sami, the Gehrys' sons, showed us around the house, Alejo assuring us that it was all right to step on a chain-link floor, while Sami pointed out the black and white Ellsworth Kelly print that hung above his bed. Walking through the house we experienced many of the elements familiar in Gehry's other designs: play between the outdoor and indoor spaces; see-through walls, floors and ceilings that created unexpected views; angled windows in curious places that produced startling reflections (of, among other things, the moon); exposed construction elements; left-over pieces of the original house, such as the partitions with square windows in the kitchen, which reminded Gehry of the work of Robert Rauschenberg; and, an outrageous cactus in the backyard, which we glimpsed through an aperture in the corrugated metal wall that ran along the side of the house.

That November the Gehrys visited us in New York. In the course of the evening Oldenburg and Gehry revived memories of a collaboration between them that might have been. Back in 1968, Oldenburg had made a series of annotated lithographs at Gemini G.E.L. in Los Angeles on the subject of monuments and buildings. This series, called *Notes,* included a proposal for the new Pasadena museum that was being planned. His design was based on an ad in the *Los Angeles Times* that showed a cigarette package and a tobacco tin. About this equation of found object with museum, he wrote:

. . . the telescoped construction suits the different scales required for a museum's functions—food, books, exhibitions and auditorium. Beautification is achieved by literal rendering of the original—its color, the revealed tobacco in relief and the ripped open silver paper of the cigarette package (a flourish). In the scale I imagine, the source of the structure would not be obviously identifiable, except from an airplane.[1]

1. From *Claes Oldenburg: Notes,* by Barbara Rose
(Los Angeles: Gemini G.E.L., 1968), brochure.

At the time it was suggested to Oldenburg that he work out the proposal with Gehry, already known as one of the few architects with a creative understanding of art. The artist did not follow up on this suggestion, partly because he had to leave Los Angeles, and partly because his architectural aspirations ended with designing the shell of a building. His ironic concept of a museum was sufficiently well expressed in a drawing, because like his other proposals for colossal monuments and buildings, this one existed in the realm of the imagination and wasn't intended to become real; he hadn't yet even been offered the chance to build large outdoor sculptures. At that time a collaboration between Oldenburg and Gehry would have become lopsided, for the artist's aim was only to propose an object that could be adapted to architecture, an attitude that left out the architect's individuality. In fact, in another page of the *Notes,* Oldenburg had even eliminated the need for architects by proposing to reduce the city of Los Angeles to alphabetical characters. He revealed his provocative attitude toward contemporary architecture in general by writing, "Why should buildings always be boxes? I suggest the use of objects as 'found' design, to construct colossal things as seriously as buildings are built. The sculptor vs. the architect."[2]

A collaboration between Oldenburg and Gehry on the development of the interior spaces of the cigarette-package museum might have been an illusory idea in 1968, but by 1982 it had become a real possibility, because the situation for each of them had changed radically.

Since 1976 Oldenburg and I had been working jointly on realizing large-scale outdoor projects, including the one hundred-foot-tall *Batcolumn* for Chicago, the *Flashlight* for Las Vegas (as tall as a lighthouse), and the fifty-seven-foot-long *Crusoe Umbrella* for Des Moines. These projects exposed us to the kinds of problems faced by architects. In locating the sculptures we had to consider lampposts, flowerpots, bus stops and other disturbing elements that litter the urban environment. Like architects, we had to take into account building codes, earthquake and hurricane regulations, and questions of structural design and engineering, all of which affected the sculpture we wanted to make.

Another similarity between our work on these large-scale outdoor projects and an architect's work is that the emphasis is on mental rather than manual activity. The initial concept for such a piece usually consists of a three-dimensional sketch casually put together from such perishable materials as cardboard and cloth; even though the directness and informality of such a sketch is desirable in developing the idea for the piece, the form of the finished sculpture has to be carefully thought out. In a process much like the one architects follow in designing a building, models are constructed, then modified and often discarded before the final design is achieved. Calculations by structural engineers are needed, and because of their size and permanence, the pieces must be fabricated by a contractor. At this stage the artist works through

2. From Oldenburg's accounts of his projects in *Object into Monument* (Pasadena: Pasadena Art Museum, 1971), p 18.

other people, just as an architect does in overseeing the construction of a house. However, there is a crucial difference: the artwork is not lived in. Habitability, in fact, is the primary obstacle to the transformation of art into convincing architecture. As Frank remarked on a later occasion, "The hardest thing is to take a tobacco tin, put doors and windows in it, and keep the quality of a tobacco tin."[3] In our work with Gehry, Claes has tried to obviate these difficulties to some extent by selecting for development into buildings objects that already have holes that could serve as windows or doors, such as a three-way electrical plug.

For his part, Gehry has always responded positively to artists' vocabularies. He is stimulated by the back and forth flow of information among different disciplines, such as science, art and architecture. Recently, he told me, "Rather than be influenced only by dead artists, as many of my colleagues tend to be, I have always felt that living artists are working on the same issues I am. Three artists I especially looked at, and still look at and learn from," he continued, "are Richard Serra, Don Judd and Claes Oldenburg." The time of our meeting [1982] was propitious, because, while Claes and I had been working on the problems of placing public sculpture in specific urban sites, Gehry had gone through a process of development, "... from never daring to venture into anything but abstraction to a concern also with representational objects."

In 1980 a group of architects who called themselves the "Chicago Seven," which included Stanley Tigerman and Stuart Cohen, organized an international exhibition based on the premise of restaging the Chicago Tribune Tower architectural competition of 1922, which had aimed at the design of the "most beautiful office building in the world." Gehry's contribution to this event was based on his vision that Chicago would eventually be demolished, and that its citizens would move to the wilderness, turning the city "into a music park in the middle of nowhere." His sketch, originally about eight by ten inches, but enlarged for the exhibition, depicts an uninhabited tower of solid concrete topped by an American eagle, a symbol that would undoubtedly appeal to a right-wing newspaper such as the *Tribune.* In Gehry's conception, the news is sent out through a computer inside the bird, making employees unnecessary. From huge spread wings hooked to both sides of the building hang hoist-type rides. People visiting the attraction camp out in tents around the base of the building.

At the time Gehry was fascinated by John James Audubon's paintings, especially those that contain beautiful foliage and small buildings in the background. For the exhibition, he tried to transform an Audubon eagle into architecture, but he found that the result lacked his own identity: "One can't just copy a style." He started over, but did not have time to work out an idea and instead sent a quick sketch, vividly evoking his concept. Gehry made his sketch in the spirit of the 1922 competition,

3. Unless otherwise noted, the architect's comments are taken from conversations with the author over the past four years.

Late Entries: Chicago Tribune Tower Competition **1980**

Sketch for *Late Entries:*
Chicago Tribune Tower
Competition 1980
pencil on paper
10¾ x 8⅛
Collection Deborah Doyle

Gehry's submission to the
exhibition is a tower with a
computerized eagle on top,
which dispenses the news.

Claes Oldenburg
Proposed Colossal
Monument for a Skyscraper
for Michigan Avenue,
Chicago, in the Form of
Lorado Taft's Sculpture,
"Death" 1968
collage
11¾ x 9¾
Collection Mr. and Mrs. Leon
M. Despres, Chicago, Illinois

which, among others, had included a proposal for a skyscraper in the form of a column by Adolf Loos, and one with a tower in the form of an Indian holding up a tomahawk, by three architects from Leipzig. But it was the knowledge that his concept would not be executed that allowed Gehry free rein.

Gehry's sketch for the eagle tower is very close to the spirit of Oldenburg's fantastic proposals for buildings and monuments. In 1967, the artist had proposed a skyscraper in the form of a clothespin to replace the existing gothic Tribune Tower, calling it a "late submission" to the original competition. Moreover, he had made another proposal for Chicago that expressed a mistrust of the computer era, similar to that inherent in Gehry's drawing; his 1968 proposal for a skyscraper for Michigan Avenue, in the form of Lorado Taft's sculpture, *Death,* compares the computer-designed John Hancock Building to the black slab behind the graveyard sculpture.

In 1981 the image of the eagle returned to Gehry's work in a sketch for the Smith House in Brentwood, California, an addition to the Steeves House originally built by Gehry in 1959. This commission required a transition zone between the conglomerate of new objects and the old house. In California such a problem is often solved by using a kind of Spanish pergola, but in this case that type of colonnade could not serve as an entry; it had to be nondirectional, with a slight focus to the right. In order to eliminate the traditional colonnade, Gehry started to transform the unfinished Audubon eagle drawing into a maquette. The eagle column was to be twelve feet high, with the bird made of broken glass. Next, Gehry started to draw fish jumping out of the water, and soon another column was planned to consist of a fish rising up, two-thirds of its length, out of the asphalt; this column was to be placed in front of the kitchen window. Unfortunately, the design was denied approval by the Bel Air Fine Arts Commission.

Earlier that year Gehry had used the image of a fish in another visionary project, a proposal for a bridge that he produced in collaboration with his friend Richard Serra for a group exhibition organized by The Architectural League of New York. (See Friedman description, page 97.)

The next year Serra and Gehry were considered separately by the city of Los Angeles, to design a proposed children's nursery to be located downtown, across from the Los Angeles Times Building. Gehry wanted to add a museum for the children. The artist and the architect decided to combine the two projects and work together. Gehry started with a fish; Serra said that he was fascinated by the idea of a coiled snake in tile, but the project did not develop beyond some scribbles on a napkin.

The following year the image of the snake turned up in a proposal Gehry made for a show held at the Leo Castelli Gallery in New York called *Follies, Architecture for the Late-Twentieth-Century Landscape.*

Gehry's contribution consisted of a design for a private park-prison in the form of a coiling snake constructed of brick, in order to give it physical solidity. This snake serves as "a warning signal to prospective burglars." Gehry described the project as follows:

It is proposed that the apprehended criminal be placed in a cage under a light-well in the center of the coiled snake. The cage can be transported to an adjoining transparent pavilion, in the shape of a fish. The form of the fish has the symbolic meaning of that famous prisoner Jonah who lived inside the whale. And then there was Pinocchio. At the owner's discretion, a mechanism can be activated which moves a car holding the cage (which in turn holds the prisoner) through an underground tunnel and into the center of the glass fish pavilion. When situated in the fish, the prisoner would be visible from the house.[4]

Gehry had obviously become fascinated by the architectural possibilities of fish and snake.

In the spring of 1983 Claes forwarded his 1968 plans of the Pasadena museum proposal to Gehry as the starting point for a collaboration of some kind. But faced with them Gehry developed a reluctance we could well understand, since to accept them would have forced him to fit into a shell he had not helped create. Finally, the Pasadena proposal seemed to all of us not fresh enough. Instead I proposed that we start from scratch by studying our respective methods.

Consequently, in August of that year Oldenburg and I went to Los Angeles to spend two weeks in Gehry's office in Venice. We studied his past projects, realized and unrealized (like the project for the Beverly Hills Civic Center), and visited the sites of as many current projects as we could, including the Aerospace Museum, on which construction had just started, and the nearly finished campus of the Loyola Law School. As we visited the different sites we came to understand Gehry's desire to make "a stronger sculptural statement of the shell," a concept which converged with Oldenburg's idea of enlarging stereotypical objects to an architectural scale. Both wanted people to be able to relate directly to the exterior regardless of the building's function. Once settled in the office, we set ourselves problems that would take Gehry's architectural approach into account: for example, we thought of a row of jars and boxes on a shelf (of the kind we had seen in his carpentry shop), a concept that would have a diffused organization and that could also deal with abstractions as representational objects. Another example of such an overall plan is a miniature golf course, which implies a consistency of apparently dissimilar things. On our Sunday outings on the Gehrys' boat we studied the Marina; its "cluster" organization and ship forms stayed in our minds, as well.

We discovered that Gehry's working method is more open than that of most architects, and allows for continuous change. As not everything is built at once, there is <u>always o</u>pportunity to adjust and change. He has the tolerance to be able to set one plastic form next to another

4. Frank Gehry, "The Prison," from *Follies, Architecture for the Late-Twentieth-Century Landscape* (New York: Rizzoli, 1983), p 51.

disparate one; this fact seemed to open up a way in which we could all work on an equal basis. We became more and more aware of the potential of working jointly on a project and all three of us were willing, as Frank put it, "to leap into the unknown," because we trusted that if we fell we would always catch one another.

A concrete result of that first visit was the *Toppling Ladder with Spilling Paint,* which Oldenburg and I conceived as a response to Gehry's methods and aesthetic, to be placed on the Loyola Law School campus in the context of an art program Gehry saw as the fulfillment of his design. In addition, there were to be a mural by Ed Ruscha on the subject of the law and stained glass windows by Jeremy Gilbert-Rolfe. Still, this was just a response, not the real collaboration we sought.

In March 1984 we made our first attempt at a real collaboration when Germano Celant organized a one-week session with students of the Polytechnical University of Milan. In view of our involvement in art and architecture we planned a project that combined both architecture and theater.[5] For our subject we chose Venice, which seemed appropriate as it is a city laid out like a stage. We selected a composite image, a red Swiss army knife, which was flexible enough to tie together the performance and the architecture, and also to reconcile historical Venice with its present status of tourist city. The knife could be used both in its normal cutting function, as the architectural theme and, in a dislocated way apart from its function, in the performance. We chose a site all three of us had strong memories of, the Arsenale, an ancient citadel and abandoned navy yard, whose oldest streets, along the Darsena Vecchia (Old Dock), date back to the twelfth and thirteenth centuries. As the first step in this "Corso del Coltello" we met on 25 March with the students and their teachers, Celant and the architect Maurizio Vogliazzo, all of whom had taken the train from Milan. We explored the site and began to gather materials related to the Arsenale and Venice, such as snapshots, stock photographs, maps and souvenirs. In venturing along the high, abrupt wall of the Arsenale, which faces the uneventful Laguna Morte, Gehry found the solution to the architectural part of the project. We could build, as an imaginary project, an entirely new section of the city in the form of a complex of islets, to begin 150 feet from the shore behind the Arsenale. This idea suited the way Venice had originally expanded along the Rivo Alto, through the addition of new city areas on the archipelago in the lagoon.

In the course of a week the students developed two models, one of the area around the Arsenale, and another, a large one, of "Coltello Island," a structure that would house about 200 artisans and provide them with facilities such as a bank, a medical clinic, a fire station and even a theater. The buildings and housing complexes could rise up, in clusters, out of the water. They would appear to be slices that together formed the island. Bleachers cut through and placed on different angles

5. The iconography of the *Toppling Ladder with Spilling Paint,* the knife image and the origins of the performance *Il Corso del Coltello* are discussed in my article "Waiting for Dr. Coltello," *Artforum,* September 1984, pp 88-92. A book on the performance *Il Corso del Coltello,* which took place on 5, 6 and 7 September 1985, in Venice, will be published in the fall of 1986.

**Il Corso del Coltello   1984
Venice, Italy**

Claes Oldenburg
*Design for a Theater Library
for Venice in the Form of
Binoculars*   1984
pencil, colored pencil, chalk,
watercolor
one-half of 30 x 40 sheet of
paper (with *Coltello/Ship*,
p 122)
Collection the artist

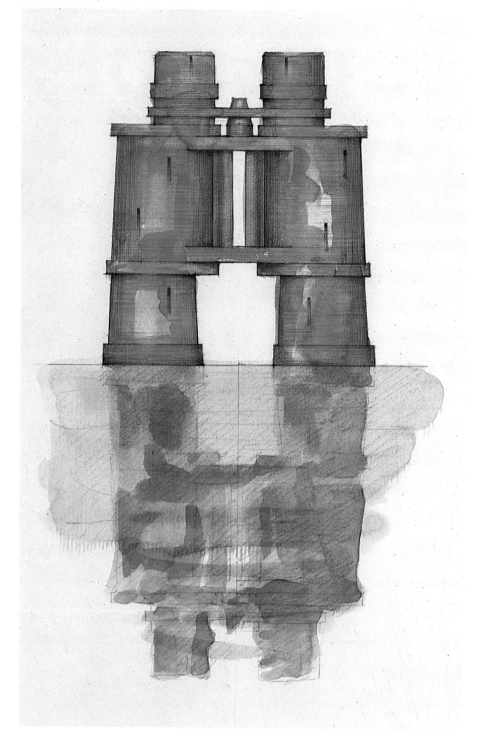

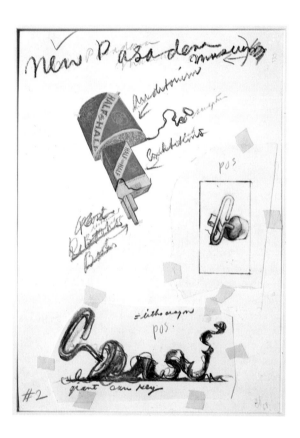

Claes Oldenburg
"Proposal for the new
Pasadena museum,"
from *Notes*   1968
lithograph
Collection the artist

A conception that might
have been the basis for a
collaboration with Gehry,
such as that now being
realized on the Main Street
project, Venice (see p 152).

Claes Oldenburg
Sketch of Frank O. Gehry's
Firestation in the Form of a
Snake, and Oldenburg's
Office Building in the Form

of a Grand Piano Lid   1984
pencil, crayon, watercolor
30 x 40
Courtesy Leo Castelli
Gallery, New York

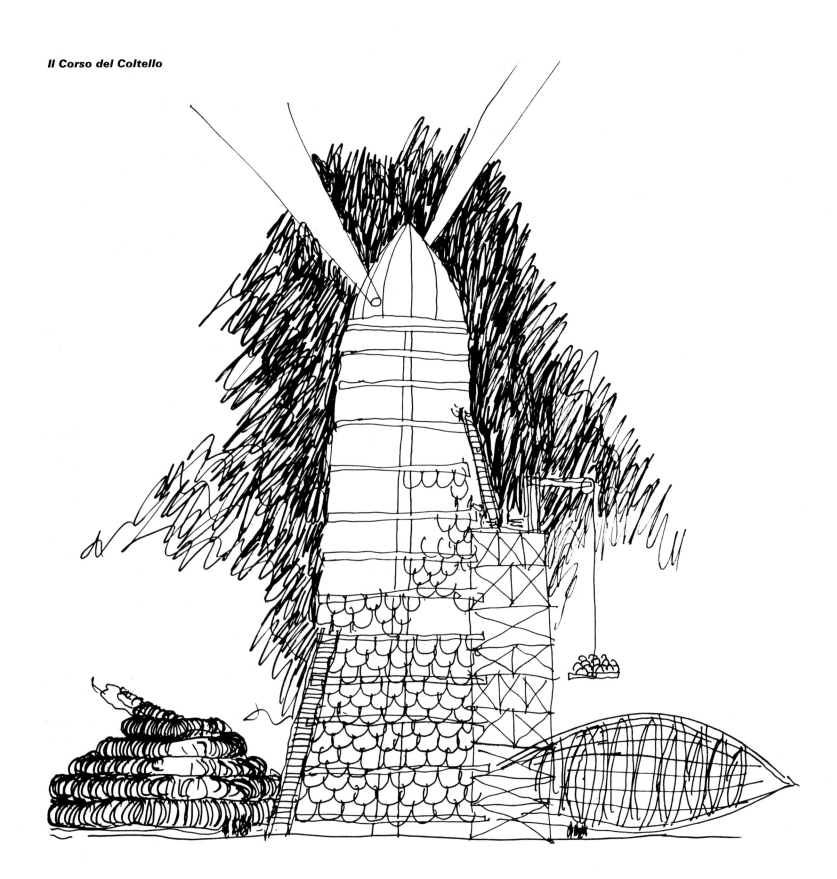

would become containers for housing. Gehry's snake turned up as a fire station, next to an office building designed by Claes Oldenburg, which was shaped like the opened lid of a grand piano.

Although this project for Coltello Island was imaginary, working jointly on it raised for Gehry, Oldenburg and me the question of how to relate sculptural architecture to a representational object that strongly determines the exterior shell of a building. First we concentrated on the theater complex. To house the library, Oldenburg suggested a brick facade shaped like a pair of binoculars. Gehry and I proposed a theater whose rear wall would serve as a drive-in movie for gondolas. The theater complex would be constructed on a platform over concrete pilings. This base—a sort of floating table—would be about four and a half feet high, which meant that a foot and a half of its height would be under the surface of the water in the shallow lagoon. The first difficulties we encountered had to do with the way the two parts would meet: in a collision, with the binoculars intruding into the room; in a clear cut; or, in a gradual transition from the object into architecture, or vice versa. In that brief time we were unable to find a satisfying balance. The facade seemed only to solidify historical overtones relating to the towers of the Arsenale and other vertical structures in Venice, while the theater made a clean break with those. The binocular facade seemed too traditional and self-contained, resisting an amalgamation with another disparate, fragmentary shape, such as the theater, which would be more open to relationships.

Shortly before leaving for Milan, Gehry had received a commission to design a camp for children with cancer, to be built in the Santa Monica Mountains. He saw this as the perfect opportunity for a real collaboration. He invited Oldenburg and me to join the design team along with Peter Walker, the landscape architect. And so, we returned to Los Angeles in April, we set aside the Venice project in order to focus on Camp Good Times. In taking on this commission we were well aware not only of its aesthetic but also of its ethical dimensions. As a result of our confrontation with and sympathy for the children's plight, we worried early on in our team meetings about the propriety of the artistic direction we were giving the project.

Oldenburg and I had a clear sense of our limitations. As Oldenburg put it, we did not have "... at our fingertips a remembered lexicon of building forms and past examples or a knowledge of materials, engineering possibilities, and costs." In our leap into architecture we relied on Frank to catch us if we fell. We resolved to think first of the children, while respecting a necessarily strict schedule and a limited budget. At the same time, we were determined not to set aside our personal interest in fusing art and architecture, but to come up with the most challenging forms we could, in the expectation that in the end this approach would yield the most beneficial environment we were capable of providing for the children. We felt also that the higher

Drawing for *Il Corso del Coltello* 1985
ink on paper
11 x 14
Collection Coosje van Bruggen

the quality of the camp, the more exposure it would get, which might in turn lead to further support for similar cancer-care institutions.

The process of developing the project for Camp Good Times was complicated by a change of site about three months after we had signed the contract. Both were located high up in the Santa Monica Mountains. The original camp site was a plateau inside the first range of mountains, a series of pastures surrounded by bushy, hilly terrain. While visiting the site in April 1984 we were struck by the intense heat and the dryness of the landscape. We felt there was an urgent need for large amounts of relieving water and shade. It seemed only natural to think of water activities such as fishing and swimming in relation to camping, and such structures as bridges and watermills, along with boats and flapping sails. This evoked the possibility of using canvas for shade. We thought of placing a lake on the plateau, with contours like those of a jigsaw puzzle piece, whose banks would range from a soft, natural edge to a hard, artificial one made of concrete. Puzzle pieces could be used as positive or negative forms; islands could be positive pieces, in the negative one of the lake.

Our plan called for entering the property through a gate below the level of the pastures. A visitor would pass a barn (an existing barn would be remodeled) and a pasture with grazing cows and horses, and then walk up to the lake where a cluster of sculptural architecture would come into view. This small village would include the dining hall, the infirmary, staff quarters and service areas. Some of the streets in the village would be waterways, and some of the buildings would rise up from the lake in a way reminiscent of Coltello Island. Near the village we laid out playing fields, while the swimming pool was to be a defined area in the jigsaw puzzle lake. Dormitories, which would be placed along the edges of the lake, would be unique in their shapes and character. In addition to the more permanent "urban" village there would be more adventurous structures at other sites. Barges would be moored on one side of the lake, recalling the houseboats that Frank Lloyd Wright designed in 1922 for the Tahoe Summer Colony. The children could spend the night on them or on land nearby, where a camp of movable tents would be located.

We did not want to create a stereotypical camp or a slice of Disneyland, but rather to offer the children new experiences they might not otherwise have an opportunity to enjoy. They could stage their own performances in a natural amphitheater on the property, make pottery, paint in a pavilion with removable walls that would be situated on a small island (reached by boat), make excursions to an observatory on top of a mountain and communicate among themselves through their own radio station and printing office. These activity stations would be located near each other, so that the children would not become too fatigued by having to walk long distances. We projected arbors, sun-shields, trellises and sprinklers to protect them from the heat. A

Camp Good Times 1984-1985
Santa Monica Mountains, California

Camp Good Times came to a painful resolution, but it started out with high hopes, as most projects do. When I was asked to design a camp for children with cancer I was terrified of dealing with that idea. I said I would consider the commission if the client would have Claes Oldenburg and Coosje van Bruggen, his wife, with whom I'd been collaborating on another project, participate in this one. I thought it was appropriate for many reasons. This kind of camp could be exciting, and it shouldn't look backwards; it should give these kids something special.

That was the intent accepted by the client, and we started work. It was a true collaboration throughout the process. Pete Walker, the landscape architect, was part of the team and we worked with a doctor, the

(above and overleaf)
Model of the Santa Monica Mountains site for Camp Good Times with all of the elements in place as they were envisioned by the Oldenburgs and Gehry. The buildings are scattered over the site in what Gehry has characterized as "organized disorder."

Camp Good Times

Model of the dining hall, entry side, Camp Good Times. The porch roof is like the skeleton of an inverted ship's hull (see entry detail, opposite, bottom).

camp director, and a conservationist who was in charge of the Santa Monica Mountains Conservancy, where the camp was to be located. So with these people looking out for all their varied interests, and us, the team became quite strong. We assigned the project to an architecture studio at Harvard, and Claes

and Coosje and I worked with fifteen students. We brought the clients to Harvard to hear the juries and participate during the process. There was a lot of discussion about aesthetics, and we talked in the early days about what constituted an appropriate image. Should this be just an ordinary camp?

Ordinary camps are very rustic and raw and we wondered if there were a need here to be different. We agonized about that in the very beginning. We were told, and we agreed, and finally felt strongly that one needn't talk down to this situation. One should really deal with the future and be optimistic; make it a good place as you would for any normal kids' camp.

We went through many iterations. There were problems with lakes because of the young children. The camp directors felt they might be too dangerous. There was a need for water up in those areas because it's very dry and very hot. With the summer sun beating down, those California hills can be very unpleasant. There weren't many trees on the site, and the water was finally excised from the project. The site was a beautiful plateau, it had rolling terrain, and we found that we could place the buildings on the terrain without major grading if we were willing to accept a scattered camp plan.

Each building and its site were carefully considered and staked out. Then the problem became, how do you relate them to the landscape without going into expensive planting, grading, catwalks, stairs, paving, all those things? How do you just naturally relate them? The issue was, were they close enough to be cohesive? Was there enough strength in them to hold, to make a space? We organized a public main space at the entry where the cafeteria, the infirmary and the counselor dorms were located. There was another zone beyond for the dormitories, and that created a space. In between, we joined it with a bridge that Coosje had designed that became the sun shade, and then there was a grove of trees planned in relation to that. So there was a transition between the two spaces, and the swimming pool was in that transition as well. The bridge became the changing rooms and storage for the swimming pool. There was an

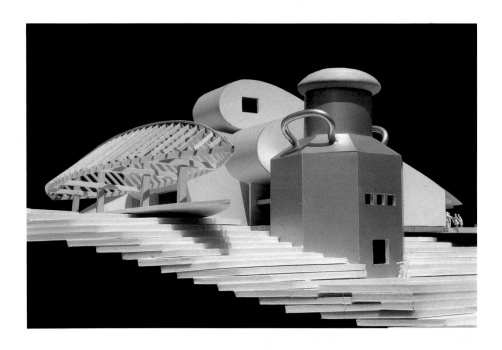

Model of dining hall for Camp Good Times seen from the side. The kitchen is in the shape of a milk can, the hall's roof a series of frozen wave forms.

Camp Good Times

amphitheater also that nestled into the hill, and an arts and crafts area. The arts and crafts were to be in small units. Claes, Coosje and I wanted to be very playful with that, and we made funny little objects. I think the building that best summarizes our design intent is the dining hall. The three of us really spent time on it and arrived at a form that grew out of our collaboration in a very natural way. Our final presentation of all these buildings to the camp administration was very pleasant until somebody from the board decided that the project was too 'arty' and that the kids really would like something more rustic—a normal camp. He suggested Huckleberry Finn as a metaphor. I think there's a kind of sentimentality in looking back to Twain that relates more to my generation than to the kids who are going to be using this camp. Anyway, that led to a changing of the architectural intent, which made it impossible for us to continue working.

preliminary model, containing the roughed-in program and space allotments, but no specific designs, was approved by the clients in July. Oldenburg and I left Los Angeles for Europe, but continued to develop ideas for the camp throughout the summer.

When we returned, Gehry informed us that a more desirable site, farther to the west and near the boundary of Ventura County, had become available. This spectacular location was on the slope of a mountain range, high above two canyons that converged toward the ocean. When the three of us next met, in February 1984, we tried to adapt our earlier ideas to the new site, but our model proved unsatisfactory, because to transfer the lake to the smaller area of the new site would have required more landfill than is allowed in the canyons. Subsequently, our clients also developed reservations about having a lake, which they considered too difficult to guard. As a result, on our return to Los Angeles in April 1985, we were faced with the fact that the lake—which had been the core of our planning—had to be nearly eliminated.

However, we were reluctant to give up the water imagery, and longed somehow to bring the ocean, which was visible at the end of the canyon, to the site. One day we imagined a tidal wave rising up to the site and receding, leaving behind debris. This vision replaced our original design with a random, playful organization more in keeping with the cascading nature around the new site, which had been formed by a landslide, setting the stage for the development of forms that mediated between abstraction and "thingness"—a mediation that we realized was the key to our collaboration.

We could scatter the buildings over the area, disparate elements that would be unified because of the theme. This was the kind of disorganized order that Frank often spoke of in connection with the natural development of the city: "The way I perceive urban experiences is in a fragmentary form which I try to express in the combination of more or less unrelated objects, which have a fundamental but not obvious relationship." This concept was close to Oldenburg's and my thinking, as well. We had recently proposed a fountain for downtown Miami in the form of a dropped bowl, with slices and peels of oranges scattered around a square.

We set about planning a schematic overall image of the camp. It would be a non-plan reminiscent of the debris left by a wave, but would still be a beautiful organization of objects in the grass. We did not want to alter the landscape, but planned walks to explore it. The lake was now reduced to two ponds, complete with ducks, at the entrance to the camp, providing a sort of "Lazy Ranch" welcome. The only structure that survived from the original plan was the covered fishing bridge, whose boardwalk was elongated into ramps to be placed next to the swimming pool. The bridge connected the two areas of the camp: daily activities took place on one side; the other side, where the dorms were located, was the resting place. The key building, as we saw it, was the dining and assembly hall, which we situated on the main promontory of the site, with a terrace overlooking the entire landscape. This building proved to be a breakthrough in our collaboration.

Our concept for the dining hall was a literalization of the wave form—an image both abstract and concrete—which was then sliced and varied by sliding the parts back and forth, up and down. The sliced, frozen waves formed a hangarlike roof for the hall. The frozen wave form was repeated in a shelter to be placed in the amphitheater and in a long dormitory that would span the canyons at the far end of the camp. The kitchen was first visualized as a bottle caught in the wave, and then developed into the shape of a milk can, to harmonize with the bucolic surroundings. It was placed next to the dining hall, anchoring the building in the slope. The entrance, in the form of a schematic house, was pitched forward, toward a porch whose roof was in the shape of the frame of an inverted ship's hull. Every building in the camp was distinguished by some sort of ocean or ship imagery, from the sails that shaded the infirmary roof to the freighterlike offices and staff quarters.

The success of all the structures—the frozen wave dining hall, the tumbling Maison Carrée-like entrance, the frame of a boat porch, the ancient Ravenna chapel-like milk can kitchen—would depend finally on our ability to transform them into universal shapes and evocative sculptural architecture with historical resonances.

Although the dining hall was accepted by the clients, differences arose about the overall design. The clients held out for a "Huckleberry Finn" atmosphere, with log cabins that we felt were unsanitary, impractical and banal. We were unable to reconcile these with our plan; our discussions with the clients reached a stalemate. For the children's sake we did not want to delay the construction of the camp because of our different approach and so, with regrets, we submitted our resignation.

It was frustrating to be interrupted before the schematic model could be developed in detail, a process that would have been a true test of our ability to work together. One way or another, we intend to realize our collaboration in an architectural context.

Camp Good Times

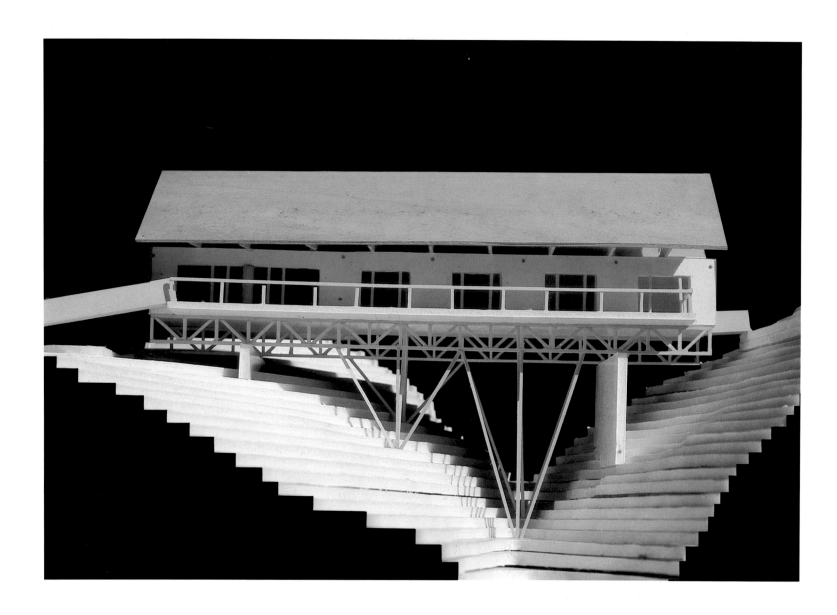

The wave dormitory would
form a bridge across a gully
in the rugged terrain of the
Santa Monica Mountains.

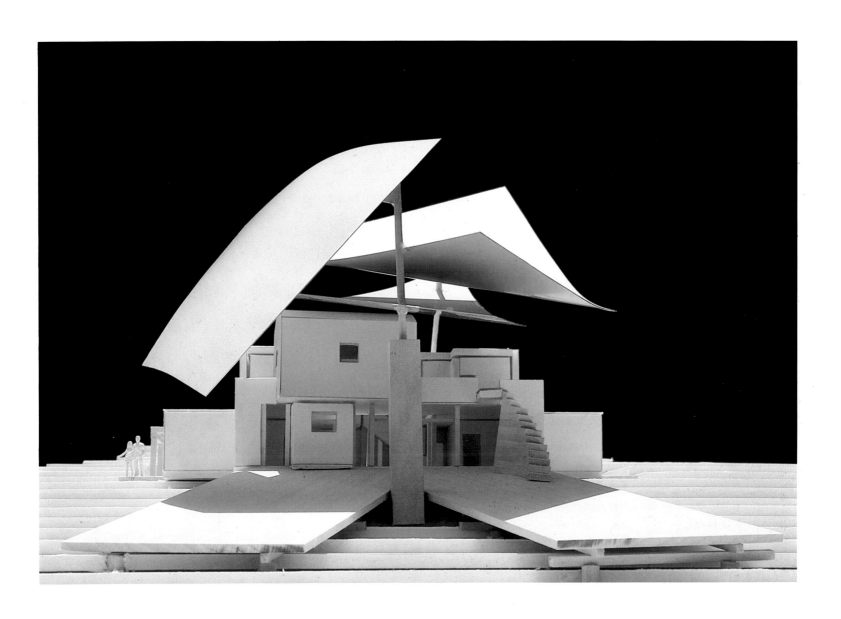

Model of the infirmary for
Camp Good Times with
flying sails designed to
provide shade. All building
forms for the camp were
based on maritime imagery.

Smith House 1981
Brentwood, California

Robert Smith and his wife, Joanne, who is a landscape architect, bought the house I did in 1959 called the Steeves House, and asked the realtor for the name of the original architect, because they wanted to extend the building. I invited them to the office and showed them that my work had changed a lot since 1959 when I was emulating Frank Lloyd Wright. Now my emulations were wider spread. I showed them the house for the filmmaker that was in process, and made them go out and look at my work. They called back and said that they'd seen all of these jobs, had been in some of the houses, had read the articles, seen pictures, and said they were still interested in pursuing the addition. There were a couple of things they didn't want us to do. They didn't like corrugated metal and they didn't like chain link. That was acceptable to me. I didn't care if I ever used those materials again, I thought. So I accepted the job. I went to visit the site several weeks later and discovered a six-foot-high chain link fence all around the site. I called Joanne Smith and said, 'How could that have happened—you told me you hate chain link?' And she said, 'Oh, well, that's just a fence around the property.'

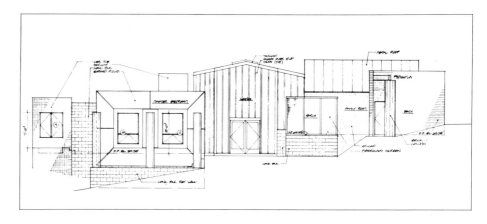

South Elevation

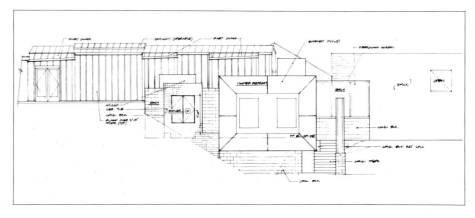

West Elevation

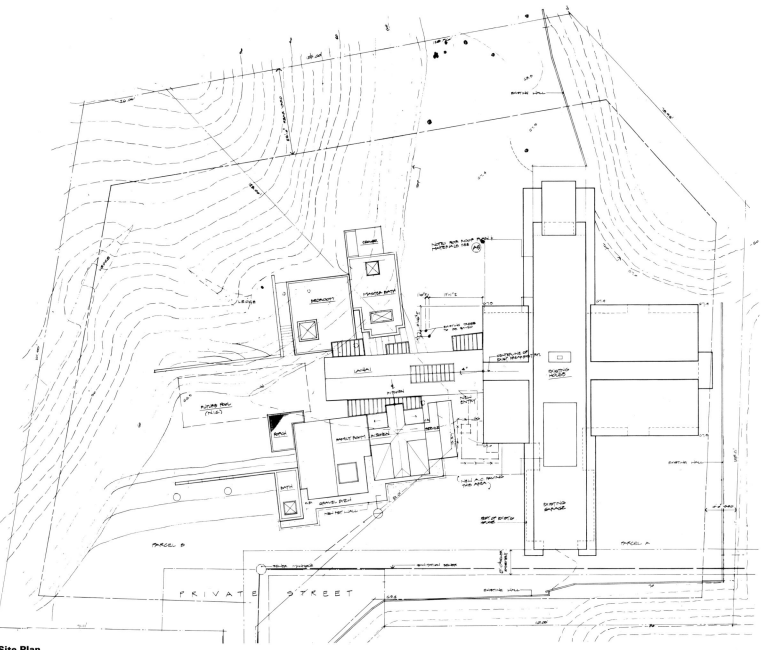

Site Plan

(opposite)
Sketch for the Smith House
addition, with proposed
eagle and fish columns to
mark the entrance. 1981
ink on paper
8⅛ x 10¾
Collection Mr. and Mrs.
Robert Meltzer

The separate objects of the filmmaker's house inevitably had to be connected. It was a logical outgrowth of that house to then take such forms and try to bunch them together, to see if the sculptural character of each piece could accrue to the adjacent ones. We made many models. I think we probably spent more time on this than our client was willing to accept, so it delayed the project a bit, but we finally got it designed and it came in close to budget.

The design was turned down by the Bel Air Fine Arts Commission as not being a house, and I think the clients really got scared. Anyway, to my regret, the project was cancelled.

Smith House

Model of the Smith House, east elevation.

(below)
Model of the Smith House site plan indicating the new buildings (attached but articulated rooms), and the existing house at right.

The original house was designed by Gehry in 1959 for the Steeves family.

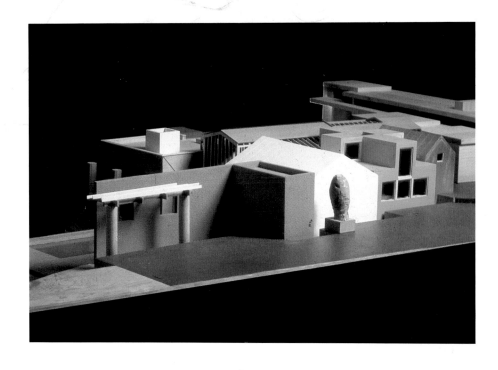

Photographs of the Smith addition model show the pool and lanai (bottom, left); the east elevation, with its proposed jumping fish sculpture (top, right); and, the southeast corner of the site with the master bedroom suite in the foreground. The freestanding columns outside the bedroom wall evoke Loyola Law School's Merrifield Hall, designed at the same time.

Médiathèque-Centre d'Art Contemporain   1984
Nîmes, France

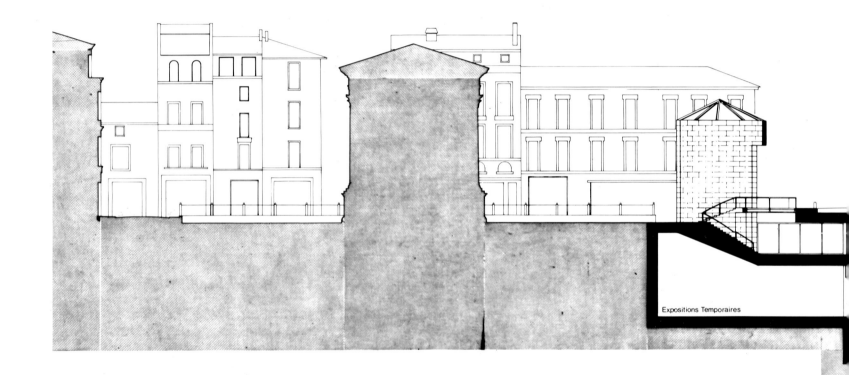

Expositions Temporaires

I realized after doing this that it's really difficult for me to work on competitions, because my process becomes so involved with the finished building that all of the drawings and debris along the way are really not finished, not resolved. Competitions require a lot of salesmanship and I was really so focused on the program and the problem and the project that our entry had to be pulled off the desk to send it out of here. It wasn't finished. There was quite a bit of logic to the project as I conceived it that just wasn't resolved enough. What the jury saw was chaos as compared to the other submissions, which were very quiet and conservative. The program as it turned out was larger than it should have been for the site. It subsequently was reduced. Had that happened earlier our

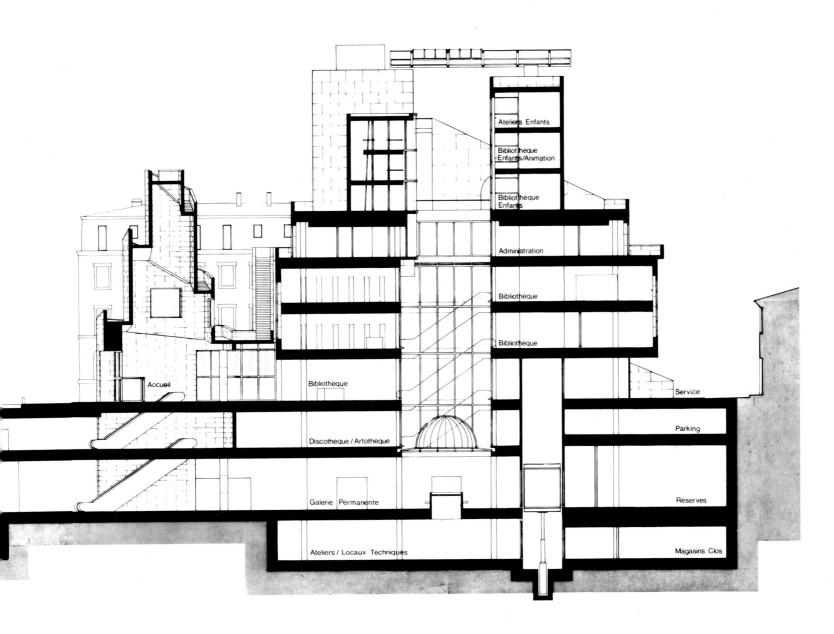

Ateliers Enfants

Bibliothèque
Enfants/Animation

Bibliothèque
Enfants

Administration

Bibliothèque

Bibliothèque

Service

Accueil

Bibliothèque

Parking

Discothèque / Artothèque

Galerie Permanente

Réserves

Ateliers / Locaux Techniques

Magasins Clos

scheme would have worked a lot better.

The mayor of Nîmes asked my team to remove the colonnade of the nineteenth-century opera house that had burned down. I told him that if that were in Los Angeles, it would be one of the best buildings in L.A. He said he'd sell it to us. So there was a kind of dismissal of that in our understanding of the project, and other architects also were apparently asked to tear it down because every project proposal did propose to tear it down. I'm not sure whether it should stay or be torn down. I sort of like it there—it completes the square and one could build a nice building behind it, but not the program that they anticipated.

Médiathèque-Centre d'Art Contemporain

The problem was how do you put something against the Maison Carrée that holds its own with that illustrious building, and doesn't become a second-class citizen in the space. The mayor said, 'Well, that was done long ago. I'm inviting architects to participate in this competition that I believe can do as well or better for its time.' So it was kind of a challenge to make something expressive of whatever we are and that held its own with the Maison Carrée. I dealt with the problem of getting people to come to the art museum. Because the collection in Nîmes is just being formed, it's not likely, as it stands, to generate a lot of traffic. People aren't going to come from all over the world to see the Nîmes art collection as it's now constituted. So I tried to deal with that problem by using the library portion of the project as the anchor tenant, in shopping center parlance. It would be one anchor, with the Maison Carrée as the other anchor. If you could create some way that people walking

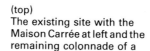

(top)
The existing site with the Maison Carrée at left and the remaining colonnade of a nineteeth-century opera house, destroyed by fire, at right.

A foam-core model from the same view as the photo above, with Gehry's proposed building in the background.

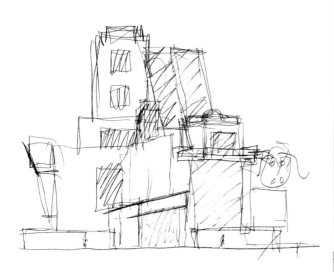

Sketch for the Médiathèque, Nîmes, entry facade with sculpture of bull's head   1984

ink on paper
8⅛ x 10¾
Collection the architect

This wooden model for the
Médiathèque is now the
property of the city of Nîmes.

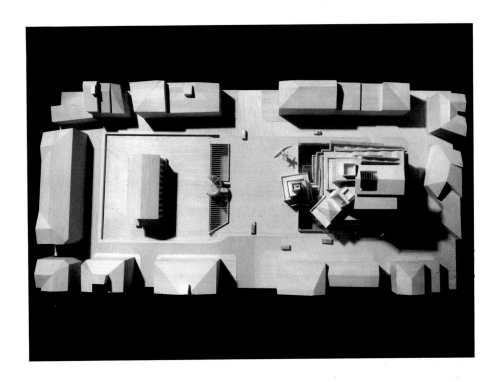

between the two would pass through the art museum, the art museum would get a lot of traffic, would become more viable and probably generate funds and contributions of art. So we proposed that the museum be underground and that the changing gallery of it be against the plaza of Maison Carrée so that people visiting the historic monument would be sucked into the museum from the plaza of the Maison Carrée. The library building was proposed to be built to the height of the cornice of the surrounding buildings, using the vocabulary of the region. I used that language to provide the children's museum and the children's library on the top with the idea that France's commitment to culture would be symbolized by its commitment to the future of culture by putting the children on top of the pile. And then we created sort of a ramp-stairway on the face of the building, diagrammatically like Beaubourg, because the one thing about Beaubourg that's exciting is watching all the people moving up and down on the building. I like the idea, I'd done it at Loyola and it really worked. I thought that the idea of kids coming and going up a ramp and going up a stairway and up to the top, would be like a mountain top. Tourists going up would come to this top terrace and look down at Maison Carrée from a new angle. The twisted corner housed the artists' studios for the children; they were twisted to face due north. At the base of that I put the director's office so that he symbolically was represented by the column of space that torqued in that space. The tradition for that is on the Champs Elysées. Its beautiful buildings go around corners and you have beautiful corner rooms that are placed at forty-five degrees to the corner, above the cornice line. I was looking at a lot of France, and I realize that the models don't look like what I'm saying, but they would have, I think, if I'd continued.

Main Street   1975-1986
Venice, California

The Main Street project's most recent metamorphosis included an entrance building in the shape of binoculars. Claes Oldenburg and Coosje van Bruggen had designed this form for the 1984 Venice, Italy project (see p 130). In its Venice, California site it will be transformed into a building

Main Street is a project that we developed ourselves, Greg Walsh and I, and we found a partner in the arrangement who would take over the whole thing—the Chiat/Day advertising agency. They are known for their inventive work—the Nike ads, beautiful billboards and their Apple computer television spots. They're a very sophisticated firm and they wanted a building that would speak to art and to an environment that their staff would work well in.

It is a difficult site, underground parking, access near the beach, the context of Venice that absorbs everything. Initially, we made three elements facing Main Street: one is a curved, boatlike shape; the center element is brick, like a cross shape, growing out of something in the Sirmai-Peterson House; and the third shape is an abstraction of tree forms, columns that we were playing with at Rebecca's restaurant. We are very excited about working on the interior systems as we haven't had a chance to do that kind of thing

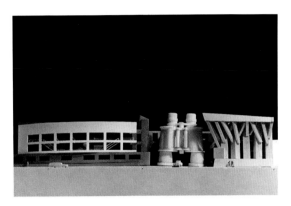

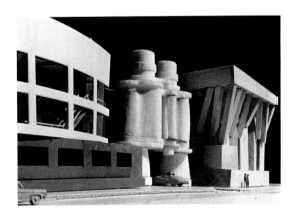

since The Rouse Company and Mid-Atlantic Toyota.

In talking about the building with Jay Chiat, he discussed wanting an art program in his building. A couple of years earlier, Claes Oldenburg, Coosje van Bruggen and I had worked with a binocular form in Venice, Italy. It grew out of an earlier idea of Claes's to have a huge binocular tower out in the lagoon. I had the maquette for the binocular tower sitting on my desk, and I pushed it in front of the central shape as I was describing to Jay Chiat

the sculptural qualities the center needed. It worked. Claes and Coosje came out to study it and felt very comfortable with it there. So we're now working on the redesign of it, to incorporate the binocular form into the entrance building, making it a functional, usable space. It takes us back to the things we were working on in Camp Good Times, and continues the process of our working together.

that will serve as the entrance to the complex and as a library for Main Street's occupants. The adjacent buildings will contain office and studio spaces for the Chiat/Day agency.

Rebecca's 1984-1986
Venice, California

Rebecca's is certainly Gehry's most flamboyant project to date. Perhaps encouraged by the success of his colorful Wosk interior (pp 182, 183) he has created an environment filled with extraordinary marine creatures—crocodiles, an enormous octopus chandelier, glass fish—and a forest of leafless wooden trees. Two private dining

Rebecca's is a small interior for a 160 seat restaurant. It's a Mexican restaurant— nouvelle Mexican. It has tacos and things like that, but haute cuisine. The Venice area has quite a few fine eateries and bars and has become a kind of yuppie hangout. I didn't want to do anything literally Mexican, but I wanted the room to have that feeling, so when you walk in you'll imagine the sound of mariachis.

We started working with onyx and now we have white, orange and green onyx. I've taken an area in the bar and used copper to create a kind of pergola. I've created a line of abstract tree forms adjacent to the bar, separating it from the dining room. The dining room is a linear, long space that goes back more than a hundred feet, and it will be lined with booths. A velvet painting by Peter Alexander will be on the wall, and in the rear of the dining space

I've incorporated the fish image—using glass this time. Fish lamps and sculptures hang from the ceiling, and over a private alcove in the rear of the dining room is a giant octopus made like a crystal chandelier. Two huge black crocodiles hang over the bar, which probably came from my experience at Nîmes, where the city hall had black crocodiles hanging in the entrance. They're made of metal with much the same technology as the fish lamps. They create indirect, atmospheric light. Walking in, you see a bunch of strange objects and forms, but the important thing I was striving for was that each element be discrete and complete, so there's no blurring. They just stand on their own in this space, and I think that's the strength of it.

rooms, one at the rear and a second on the mezzanine, will give this small restaurant a clublike atmosphere.

Yale Psychiatric Institute   1985-1986
New Haven, Connecticut

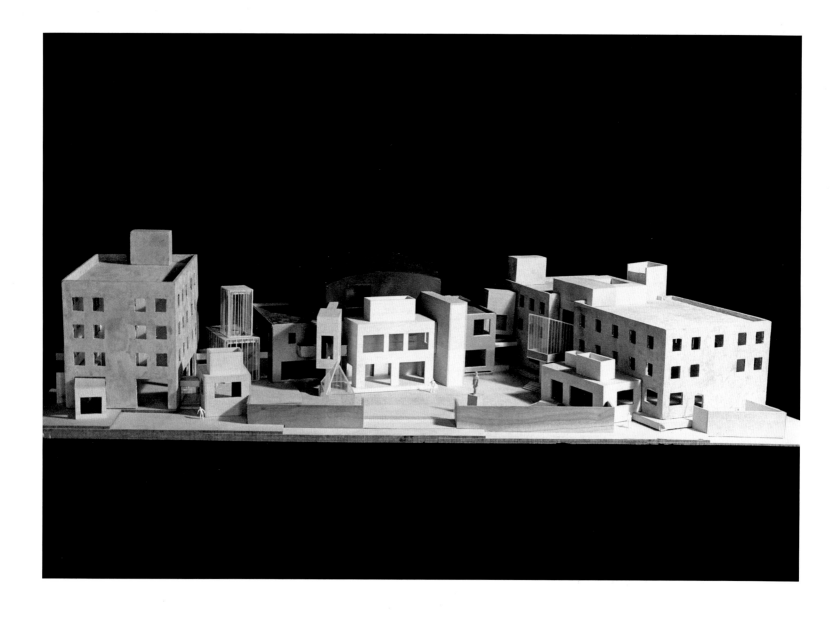

Gehry has created a townscape for the Yale Psychiatric Institute as he did for the Loyola Law School campus. These photographs of the model show the project in development, April 1986.

This building has a very tight budget, a tough context—among buildings by Louis Kahn, Philip Johnson and Kevin Roche—and a very complicated program. It is to house over sixty beds for adolescent schizophrenics, two-thirds of whom have to be restrained or secured, because of what they might do to themselves, more than what they would do to anyone else. It's a very difficult problem. I would say that working on the camp for children with cancer and the building for schizophrenic adolescents at the same time, made for some difficult days for me, especially since I have young children of my own.

The YPI sits in a transition zone between a ghetto neighborhood and the Yale Medical School. It's not a very likely space for a facility of this kind. Most new psychiatric facilities are out in the country. But at Yale, because of the necessity to be close to the school of psychiatry, the Institute had to be close to the campus, and this was one of the only sites available. The problem posed is how do you make a place for people dealing with that problem? How does it become a pleasant and relatively normal experience? How do you place such a facility into an urban neighborhood without putting a big wall around it, making it look like an asylum?

Yale's philosophy of treatment involves looking back to normalcy immediately. The minute patients arrive they're given clues to the first step back. This idea led me to the conclusion that if a portion of the ground floor could be used for commercial facilities, such as a coffee shop or a bookstore in conjunction with the entrance to the building, it would diffuse the institutionality of the entrance. It would be easier to walk into a building with people in a shop at the entrance. The store would fuse with the program of work adjustment in which the patients who are almost ready to go back into the world have the opportunity to work. The planning strategy of this project is to follow the Yale format of buildings that surround courtyards, breaking down the scale by not making it a single building, but a series of parts, so that it becomes a village with bits and pieces of varying scale (rather like Loyola) so that kids looking out their windows feel as though they're part of a space and part of a village. Through adjacency the pieces relate back to the city they're part of. Architecturally it has the same philosophy as the treatment program.

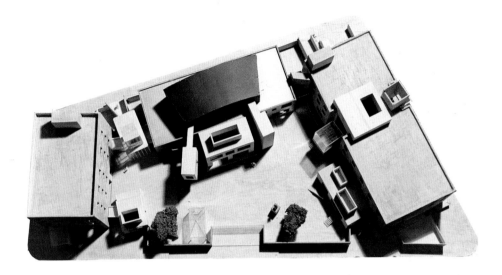

Pilar Viladas

The 1980s

The last four years have seen both a sharp rise in Frank Gehry's profile on the American scene and a marked shift in his work away from the formal vocabulary for which he is so well-known. While his projects of the 1970s and early 1980s revealed a preoccupation with exposing structure and building process—based in part on Gehry's conviction that most buildings look better unfinished—the more recent work focuses on the manipulation of discrete architectural objects. His buildings no longer look as if they are in a perpetual state of construction (or de-construction). Gone, for the most part, are the exposed wood studs, chain-link fencing and transparent layers of skeletal wall that characterize projects such as his own house, the Gemini G.E.L. building, the Spiller House, the unbuilt Familian House, and the Cabrillo Marine Museum. Instead, "finished" shapes—recognizable, if distorted, geometric solids and abstracted, archetypal building forms—either "collide" to form a single, sculptural object, or are arranged individually in a "landscape." "Collision" buildings may have distinct exterior components, but continuous interior spaces, as in the California Aerospace Museum or the Wosk Residence. In contrast, the "landscapes" take what is traditionally a single building with multiple rooms (a house, school or factory) and break it down into a number of one-room buildings arranged in a villagelike composition.

Neither of these approaches is new to Gehry. The idea of collision has figured prominently in his work since the early 1970s, illustrative of the fragmented nature of contemporary life and culture. The notion of objects-in-a-landscape first appeared in Gehry's work as early as his unbuilt Jung Institute project of 1976, and in residential works of the late 1970s and early 1980s such as the House for a Filmmaker, the Benson House, the Indiana Avenue Houses, and the unbuilt Smith House, but didn't assume large-scale built form until Loyola Law School. With this vocabulary of formal elements, both approaches lend them-

South facade by day,
California Aerospace
Museum

California Aerospace Museum   1982-1984
Los Angeles, California

The California Aerospace Museum came to us through the state of California. We were asked to design a building for which there was no budget for interiors. The entire budget for the building was $3.4 million and it could not be exceeded. We studied several strategies for placement within the overall plan of Exposition Park. It seemed that the best thing to do, since it was to be very tiny to begin with, was to attach it to the old armory building, which had considerable under utilized existing space that could be remodeled to become the future museum. So this then made our building an identification of and entry into the armory that would constitute the majority of the future air museum.

The client asked that our building symbolize the aerospace industry, because it was going to be used to attract endowment funds from it. As so much of the industry is located in southern California, this seemed long overdue.

We decided that we would start by putting objects (or buildings) around the armory so that in the future the armory building wouldn't need to be completely resurfaced. The sculptural pieces could edit the views of the old armory building to make it more powerful and more exciting. That was the way we started. The subsequent additions were the IMAX theater, which didn't come out so well, and the terrace.

The building was conceived as a giant hangarlike space, sculptural in its character, inside and outside. It was intended that the interior space be continuous. When it was all framed and enclosed for the first time the inside space was quite spectacular. It was the closest thing I'll ever get to designing a gothic cathedral. The building's interiors have since

selves to the kind of "undesigned" architecture that, for Gehry, best addresses the ad hoc nature of the American city and the texture of contemporary culture. They can be used to create the "casual" arrangements or apparent accretions of form that are the foundation of Gehry's inclusivist approach to the issue of context and which reflect his preference for what he calls "invisible" architecture. The landscape approach also affords him the opportunity to experiment with the one-room building, a problem that fascinates Gehry as it has fascinated other architects from Brunelleschi to Philip Johnson.

It is convenient that the two largest and most visible of Gehry's recent built works—the California Aerospace Museum (1982-1984) and Loyola Law School (1981-1984), located just a few miles apart on the fringes of downtown Los Angeles—offer telling examples of collision and landscape, respectively. In fact, they probably represent Gehry's best built effort in each category. Both are institutional projects with tight budgets, a condition that never seems to cramp Gehry's style, and their high visibility and urban context make their successes and shortcomings all the more significant.

The Aerospace Museum is located in the northeast corner of Exposition Park, a large tract of land that houses a motley array of civic buildings, including the Memorial Coliseum, the Sports Arena, a large rose garden, and several museum buildings ranging in style from Spanish-influenced Beaux-Arts to Contemporary Brick Box. Conceived as the first phase of a project that will eventually incorporate the classically-influenced former armory on its north side, Gehry's building, which faces a pedestrian mall, also serves as a "billboard" for the entire museum. The building itself is a near-collision of a relatively plain stucco box and an enormous, metal-clad polygon, mediated by a large, glazed wall and crowned by a triangular windowed prism and a metallic sphere. The most outrageous element of this billboard facade is the Lockheed F104 Starfighter jet that hovers, frozen in mid-takeoff, over a forty-foot-high sliding "hangar" door, announcing the museum's function in no uncertain terms. (Gehry would have preferred a German Messerschmitt, but the museum's substitute produces the desired effect.) Dynamic, forced-perspective fire stairs jut out from the polygon and from the more prosaic block of the stucco box's east end. A curving ramp leads from the south (mall) facade, around the polygon, to the north side of the building, where the entrance is located, just opposite the planned entrance to the armory building; the two entrances face each other across a narrow "street." At this point, the metallic sphere springs into focus, rendering the "back" of the building as spectacular as its billboard front. The entrance itself is a greenhouse structure similar to those used by Gehry at Santa Monica Place, Loyola Law School and the Wosk Residence. Inside the museum, the soaring, open exhibition space, with its central, ziggurat-shaped circulation core and multi-level displays, is flooded with light from the industrial-scale succumbed to the circumstance of a design firm brought in, after the fact, to design the exhibition. It was decided, in somebody's wisdom, to close off one end of the building and turn it into a theater, and they chose the most exciting space, the polygonal space, for that. It broke my heart. However, the space is still there, and someday it will open up again.

Obviously I was exploring disparate sculptural forms placed beside each other, and the sculptural qualities accruing to each from the adjacent pieces. So they are not so much in collision here as in a kind of positioning relationship to each other. They are rather like Loyola where the parts are placed next to each other, like the Smith House. I don't see them colliding so much as just gently touching each other. I really enjoy the awkwardness with which they touch, as it reminds me of the cities we live in and the kind of awkwardnesses of city buildings sitting next to each other.

It should be noted that this building as it now exists is not in its final setting; the street in front is intended to be enclosed and to become a pedestrian mall. The old buildings across the road that are part of the California Museum of Science and Industry are also to be embellished with sculptural forms placed in front of them as a means for expansion. If I were to do it all I would have a strange parade of forms down the mall and around the rose garden. I don't know whether that's going to happen, but that was the scenario discussed with the group of consultants involved. It was based on that scenario that I designed the aerospace building. Since the other parts haven't been done, my building may appear a little strange to someone not understanding the overall context.

skylights and windows that Gehry skillfully placed throughout the building. As in so many of his projects, this also means that you can see several parts of the building's "colliding" exterior elements from the interior, which is as continuous as the exterior is articulated. Gehry designed the interior as a single, hangarlike space; unfortunately, the museum's exhibition designers, over the architect's protests, walled off the interior of the polygon, effectively obliterating any sense of it from inside the building.

The Aerospace Museum is just one element in an already crowded park landscape, but even so, it is a gregarious front man for the ensemble of old and new museum buildings, including the octagonal IMAX theater (also by Gehry) to the east, and the outdoor aircraft display to the northeast. It is also the most theatrical of Gehry's built works, and it may ultimately be more exuberant than resolved. The jet plane on the mall facade is an inspired piece of advertising, yet without it, the facade would look strangely mute. And while the gray metal-clad polygon is visually compelling both up close and at a distance, it looks as if it had gone directly from schematic model to built object. Its vast expanses of monochromatic surface seem too opaque; you want to punch a few more windows in it. Similarly, you long to slide open the big hangar door, to let people stream in and out from the mall; so, no doubt, does Gehry, but the museum administration would probably take a dim view of any such initiative. It's an unfortunate fact of the planned two-building program that the entrance to Gehry's building is its back door. The mall and the front of the museum would benefit enormously if that side were open to museum visitors.

But whatever problems there are with the individual pieces of the composition, its success as a whole is indisputable. The building's muscular strength not only compliments the austerity of the old armory, while creating a badly needed presence on the mall, but it also achieves the mysterious, factorylike quality that Gehry sought for it. His combination of the tough, minimalist forms of industrial architecture and fantastically over-scaled geometric solids evokes our collective romantic image of flight and space exploration, and creates a museum building whose outside is as much a part of the exhibition as its inside.

If Aerospace represents Gehry's boldest attempt at collision, Loyola Law School is his most successful example to date of the objects-in-a-landscape approach. Given an urban campus of no distinction whatever, and an expansion program that included faculty offices, classrooms, lecture halls and a chapel, Gehry saw the opportunity to test his vision of "a pileup of buildings, like an acropolis." The classical simile took on added meaning when the client specifically asked for a campus that had a sense of place and a design that referred to the ancient traditions and architecture of the law.

The architect's proposal satisfied both his client's wishes and his own. Rather than housing the different programmatic functions in a

California Aerospace Museum

South facade at dusk.

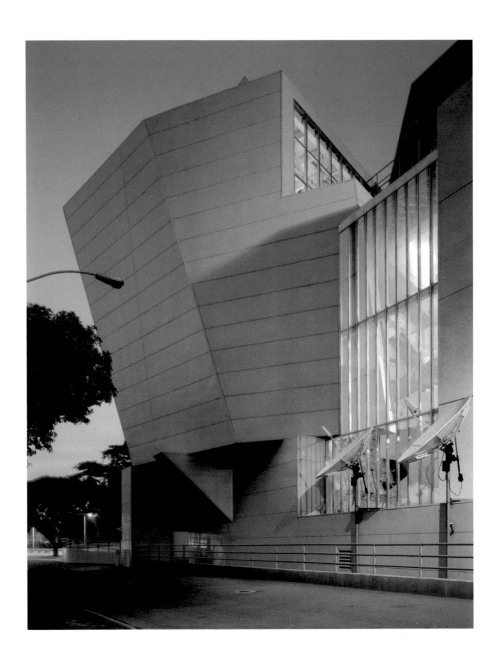

(left, top)
The junction of the existing armory and the Aerospace Museum form the museum's entrance.

(bottom)
The Museum seen from the rose garden in its Exposition Park site.

Night view, looking north.

California Aerospace Museum

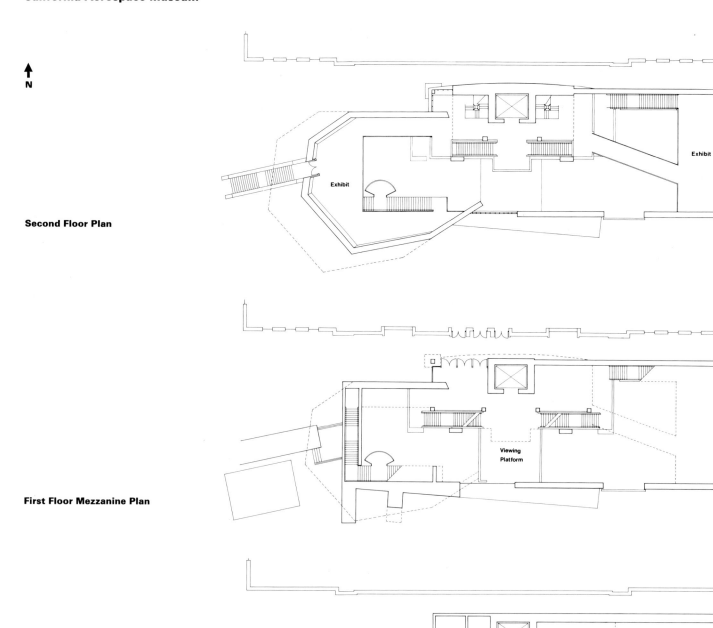

N

Second Floor Plan

Exhibit

Exhibit

First Floor Mezzanine Plan

Viewing
Platform

First Floor Plan

Exhibit

Sketch for California
Aerospace Museum   1982
ink on paper
11 x 14
Collection the architect

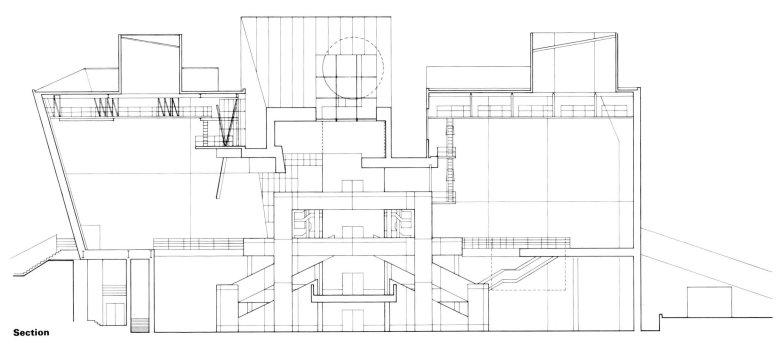

Section

**California
Aerospace Museum**

The west elevation of the
Aerospace Museum with its
ramped exit from the
primary exhibition space.

Aerospace interior with
mezzanine viewing platform
at center.

Loyola Law School 1981-1984
Los Angeles, California

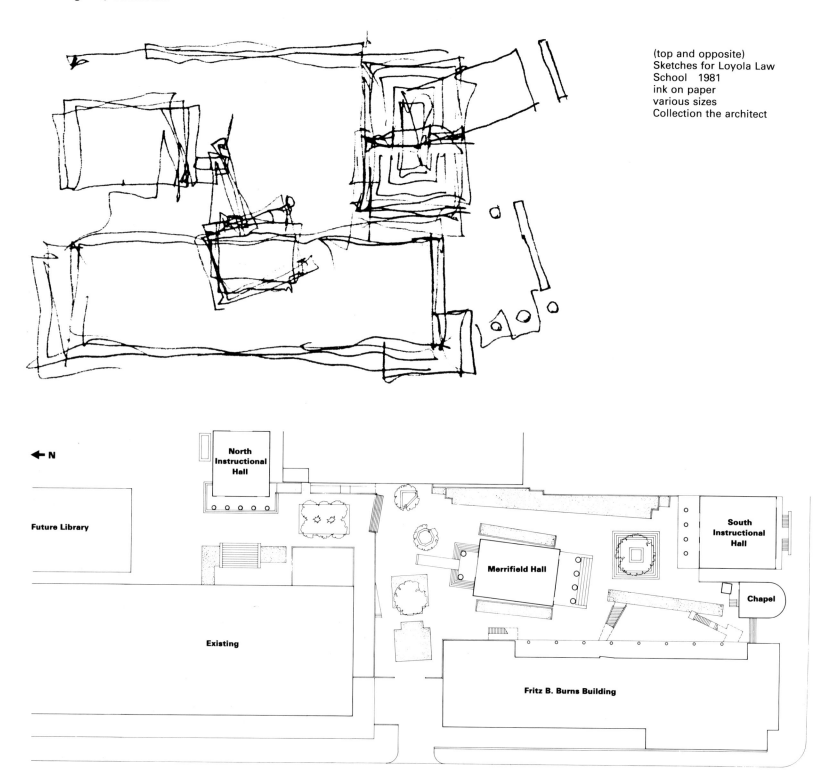

(top and opposite)
Sketches for Loyola Law
School 1981
ink on paper
various sizes
Collection the architect

← N

Future Library

North
Instructional
Hall

Existing

Merrifield Hall

South
Instructional
Hall

Chapel

Fritz B. Burns Building

Site Plan

This was the kind of project I'd been wanting for a long time. I went to the interviews fully expecting not to be chosen because of the seemingly conservative character of the client. I was very surprised when our office was chosen. I was very excited about this project because it was in town, in a rough neighborhood, but a neighborhood I knew from the years when I lived three blocks from the site—my first abode in southern California in 1947. I met with faculty and students, and faculty committees and student committees and trustee committees, and the overall issue—the central theme that kept coming back—was the need to create a place in this funny wasteland that didn't upstage the neighbors. Because the neighborhood was part of the Catholic Archdiocese, it was felt that it should not be overwhelmed by this project.

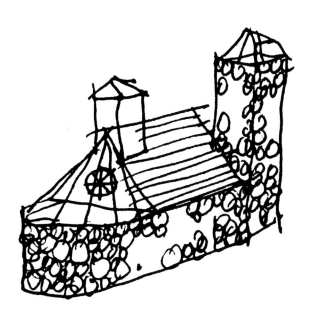

single, large building, Gehry placed the offices and classrooms in a narrow, three-story building, and the chapel and lecture halls each in one-room buildings. The result is a miniaturized urban piazza, in which the larger structure, the Fritz B. Burns Building, serves as a foil for the smaller ones, which are placed "casually" around the courtyard in front of it. From the main entrance on Olympic Boulevard, little of the campus is visible until you climb the few steps that lead up to it. There, the Burns Building's long, yellow stucco facade—punctuated by rows of rationalist punched windows (shades of Aldo Rossi), cleft by a skewed greenhouse atop a twisting, baroque central stair, and adorned at either end by jitterbugging metal fire stairs—is both backdrop and reference point. The static quality of its smooth surface balances the energetic motion of the elements that emerge from it, not least of which is the steady stream of students and faculty that travels up and down the central stair, spilling out into the courtyard below. In front of Burns are arrayed the three smaller buildings. Merrifield Hall (intended as a moot court, but now a lecture hall), a gabled brick box with a detached screen of fat concrete columns, is rotated a slight but crucial seven degrees off axis; the rotation gives the building greater sculptural power, and charges the entire courtyard composition with a spatial tension it wouldn't otherwise have. Opposite Merrifield Hall, with their backs to Olympic Boulevard, are the South Instructional Hall, a gray stucco box with a two-story column-and-lintel facade of galvanized metal, tough as nails and mysterious in its play of light and shadow, and the chapel. A child's drawing of a Romanesque church and campanile, it is built of glass and a Finnish plywood, normally used for concrete formwork, that is one of Gehry's more recent banal-to-beautiful material transformations. The deliberate detachment of the concrete and galvanized metal column screens from their prosaic "boxes" ensures that neither Merrifield Hall nor South Instructional Hall has a purely frontal quality (the chapel, designed by Gehry as a "piece of furniture," does not have that problem). The skewed axes, foreshortened vistas and relentless spatial shifts produce a series of constantly changing urban fragments, thus suggesting that this tiny town square evolved over time, as did the neighborhood around it. In this sense, Loyola and Gehry's other "landscape" projects can be seen as another manifestation of his concern with process—or at least the representation of it. In Loyola, we are shown the "weaving" of the urban fabric, just as Gehry's earlier "skeletal" buildings make us aware of the process of building. The idea of Loyola as an "unplanned" accretion of buildings gives its density more authenticity, enhancing its sense of place.

Loyola also raises the issue of historicism in Gehry's work. He is no stranger to historical allusion (see the column capitals in his 1963 Kay Jewelers store), but Loyola is his most overtly historicist project to date. He considers the client's preference for classical architecture more a rationalization after the fact than a valid defense of his design

Loyola Law School

The Burns Building, seen from the east.

(far right)
The Burns Building and Merrifield Hall, looking north (above).

South Instructional Hall seen from the Burns Building arcade.

(below)
The Loyola model, looking
south.

I chose to build a very simple block in which the faculty offices and student functions could be housed. The back side of it facing the street is very recessive so that it doesn't push the adjacent buildings. In fact, by association with the more complicated existing law school building, this simple building next to it enriched the old building and made the street more habitable.

I've been criticized for that by a few people who've said that I should have given more to the street, but in that neighborhood it didn't seem appropriate to build a little plaza out on the corner or a major entry plaza because it would have told a lie. The school didn't want to invite people in. They really wanted to keep the neighbors out, but they wanted it to look friendly to the neighborhood. For security reasons they had me put a fence around the site. I had to walk a tightrope between visual accessibility and the relationship to the street. Still, it isn't a solid wall; people can look in and even walk in but they really aren't supposed to.

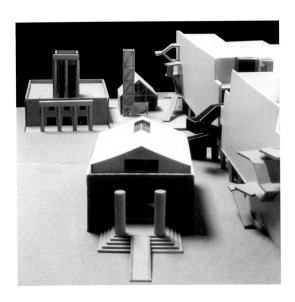

Loyola Law School

Sketches for the Loyola
campus include the Burns
Building, a schematic study
of cubistic forms (opposite),
and a study for Merrifield
Hall   1981
ink on paper
various sizes
Collection the architect

I chose to take the classroom buildings out of the main building because had they been there, the clear span of the main building would have been more expensive. This way I was able to take the money I saved and use it to embellish the little buildings, give them more character, and create a campus. I tried to stay away from tricky site plans so that the Burns Building is against the street and on the southern portion the classroom building and

chapel form an L and enclose the campus, with space between so you can see in. It was a simple, ordinary site plan I was trying to achieve. I didn't want it to be a self-conscious design. And then I put the building in the middle that was supposed to be the moot court, but later was converted into a classroom and robbed of its symbolic stature. The change was made during construction so it was too late to do anything about it. I tilted

that building seven degrees to the grid to separate it and give it more importance, and to increase the tension between the parts. In the large Burns Building I took the stairways that would normally have been inside and spilled them onto the outside of the building with the idea that it would animate the facade and bring people out onto the front of the building. That does work. When classes break you see the front of the building covered with people running up and down the stairs. That complements the people walking around in the space below and gives it a lot more excitement. Keeping the stairs on the outside was cheaper than putting them inside because it was more like a fire escape. You weren't buying the enclosure of so much space. So it was a cost-saving strategy as well.

The main wall of the Burns Building I painted a bright color, treated it like a stage set against which the smaller classrooms and the people played. And that was internalized to the court so you don't see that so much from the outside.

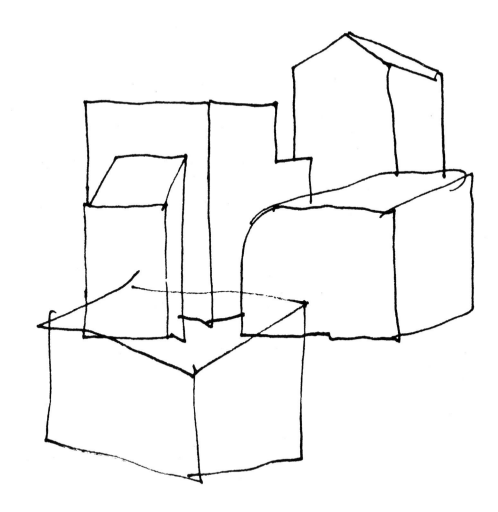

Loyola Law School

We designed the buildings and the landscape. I decided to continue the informal strategy by placing pieces of green, like objects, and separate tree objects to complement the freestanding columns at a different scale and texture. The total composition—I guess one could make analogy to Eastern composition rather than Western composition—was somewhat random although each piece was very carefully thought out and scaled and designed and placed. The main thing about Loyola, the most difficult thing was to try to achieve so much with so tight a budget—one of the most difficult budgets I've ever had.

We are getting ready to start an additional phase—we've now done three phases—the original Burns Building, the classroom buildings and the courtyard, and then remodeling the interior of the original building as a library. The fourth and fifth projects are to build recreational facilities on the Olympic Boulevard side—east of the project—and to tear down the warehouse building on the north side in the site plan, which on our drawings is referred to as future library. There we will make some kind of publications-law review building that will

become an entry from 9th Street, because many people park up at that end and come in that way. That will complete the picture until such time as the parking garage is dealt with. It will be a complete campus in the next few years.

Loyola's chapel, by day and by night.

(opposite)
South Instructional Hall (left) seen with the chapel and Burns Building, looking south.

Norton House   1983-1984
Venice, California

My pride and joy. It was designed at the same time as the Wosk Residence. The budget was very, very tight—and maybe that's what I'm best at. In this project I was dealing with the complex context of Venice. Anything you put in Venice is absorbed in about thirty seconds—nothing separates itself from that context. There's so much going on—so much chaos. In the Norton House we were trying to get into that, trying to figure out how to co-opt it, how to make a piece that would be seen, have its own integrity sculpturally, and yet become part of that cacophony.

The husband is a screenwriter, the wife is an artist. I dealt with their needs and the husband's yearnings for a private perch in which to write. He happened to mention his early days as a lifeguard and how he liked sitting in the lifeguard tower. So I picked up on that. I'm sure he never expected what he got, but I think it plays with his fantasies—that's something I like to do. There's tile on this building because I was working with it on the Wosk house—I was right in the middle of "tile-o-rama" there, and I was having so much fun with tile that I decided to use it here. Of course, the budget was very tight, so we used standard kitchen tile in the Norton House.

Spatially, I organized the interiors in relation to the ocean to give privacy, but also to provide a lot of terraces fronting on the ocean view. This particular beach gets a lot of pedestrian traffic so the main living room terrace is set above the beach in such a way that passersby can't see onto the terrace. There's a decent level of privacy in this building.

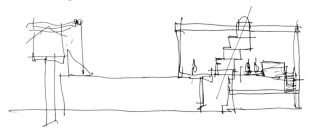

motives, since his real goal was to capture the arrangement of forms, rather than the details of the forms themselves, in these historical models. It just happened that his vision of an acropolis or the Roman Forum meshed with the Law School's classical leanings, and to dwell on the particular historical sources of the design would be to miss its point. It is the organization and manipulation of sculptural forms, much more than the stylistic vocabulary, that gives Loyola its power. Given the confused state of the architectural profession on this topic, one of Loyola's most poignant lessons is its demonstration of the essential futility of the modern/postmodern argument. Gehry's effective use of minimalist, yet archetypal, building forms proves that "abstraction" and "meaning" are not mutually exclusive terms, and that it is indeed possible to evoke the architectural past without resorting to literal quotation.

Gehry's most important contribution here, however, is in the realm of urban design. Loyola is a private institution, and for reasons both of internal security and external diplomacy, it wanted a campus that was inwardly complex but outwardly self-effacing. So, while Gehry's courtyard composition is as arresting as any he has ever designed, it blends adroitly into the jumble of low-rise commercial buildings, houses and billboards that make up the neighborhood, by presenting a public face that is open, but not *too* open. The South Instructional Hall and the chapel show solid backs to Olympic Boulevard, and with the anonymous street sides of the Burns Building, form a gateway that is neither forbidding nor overly welcoming. It is simply there, like everything else in the neighborhood. Loyola maintains the fabric of its surroundings while it provides one of the city's most rewarding urban spaces, and it is precisely this blend of formal power and urbanistic integrity that make it Gehry's most important built work so far.

Gehry's best-known residential projects from this period are the Norton House in the beach town of Venice, and the Wosk Residence, several miles (and a whole world) away in Beverly Hills. They are among the few recent Gehry residential works that can be evaluated fairly, since relatively few have actually been completed. And both are interesting in that they represent hybrids of collision and landscape, designed to deal with the peculiar conditions of their sites.

Less a collision than a simple stacking of programmatic elements, the Norton House (1983-1984) occupies a typically skinny site on the Venice boardwalk, one of the more colorful stretches of blue-chip real estate on the West Coast. While the clients wanted access to the ocean view, they also wanted privacy from passersby, as well as from their neighbors on the north and south. Gehry's solution was to raise the living and bedroom areas above street level by setting them on a ground floor base—the swimming-pool-blue tiled "box" that contains Mrs. Norton's studio in front and the garage on the back (alley) side. The deep second floor terrace serves as a visual buffer between the living-

(opposite)
Sketch for Norton
House   1983

ink on paper
8⅛ x 10¾
Collection the architect

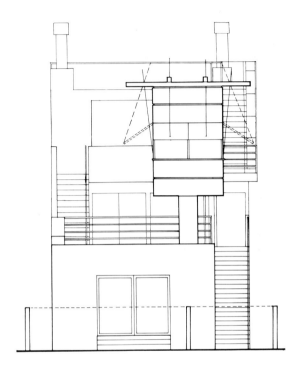

West Elevation

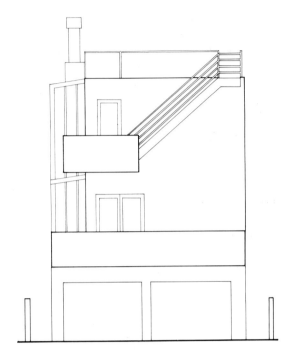

East Elevation

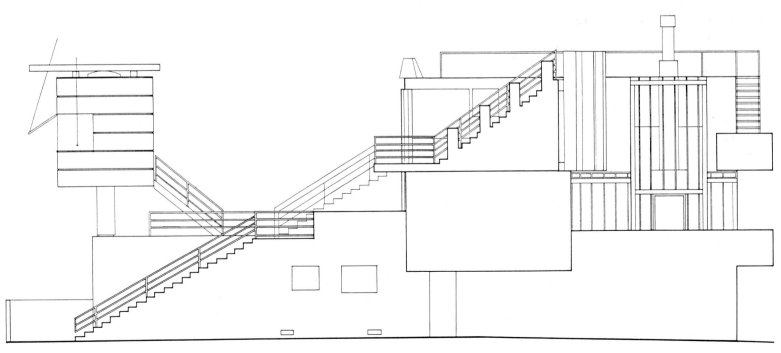

South Elevation

Norton House

(top)
The Norton House from a neighbor's roof, looking north.

(below, left)
The rear of the house with the double garage and a balcony above.

From the living room one looks over the terrace, past the owner's lifeguard station-inspired study to the ocean.

(left, top)
The Norton House, looking east. Exterior materials are as diverse as those of the neighborhood: concrete block, glazed tile, stucco and wood, all seem fitting on this narrow beach-front lot.

(left)
The Norton House stairway to the living room terrace. Ceramics on the pedestals above may someday be replaced with sculpture.

From the living room terrace there is a compelling view of the Pacific through the study.

**Wosk Residence   1982-1984
Beverly Hills, California**

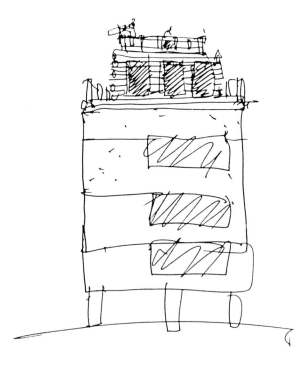

The client is an artist who had done some work that was intriguing to me. It had strength, and I saw a personal struggle in it that was dealing with a rather sleazy art deco—I don't know how to describe it—glitzy. We were doing a studio for the client, and the place was to be used by her and by her parents who would visit from Vancouver. They collected Israeli artifacts and were very involved with Israel. Their yearnings were different from hers. And I saw that and tried to use it in the creation of this project. I took these diverse ideas and put them together, and if they collided, let them collide. We drew from all of their images, and an early model, the first one I showed them, had many of the pieces and parts of images that they had given me. That's where we started, resolved it from there, and simplified it, to create the village on the roof that would read as discrete pieces, but that would be continuous spatially and that would join each piece in whatever awkwardness would come from that placement. This was obviously an

dining-kitchen areas and the boardwalk, but it also makes for a mighty long stretch of narrow interior space that is unbroken by glazing except at the ocean and alley ends. A deep kitchen skylight does, however, offer visual access to the third floor (where the bedrooms are located), and helps somewhat to open up the space.

But if the interiors of the house are, by Gehry standards, unremarkable, the exterior shows the architect at his contextual best. The zany pileup of boxy forms, stairs and "mismatched" materials, topped by the detached study in the shape of a lifeguard's tower (an allusion to the client's old lifeguard days) and the red chimney, seen through the "sheared away" south wall, look right at home among the "dingbat" bungalows and shingled shacks that line the boardwalk. Outrageous as the house appeared in model form, you can easily walk right past the real thing.

The Wosk Residence (1982-1984), on the other hand, is hard to miss. It's the only penthouse village in Beverly Hills, and since it's just four floors up, it makes a big impression. The top floor of a duplex apartment (the building's original fourth floor was demolished to make room for the new "roofscape"), Gehry "borrowed" forms, both from the neighborhood and from more exotic locales, to create his version of the little buildings you might see cluttering any urban rooftop. Given the low and distinctly uncluttered scale of Beverly Hills, the metaphor is a bit tenuous, but then this isn't exactly a strict exercise in contextualism. A ziggurat coated with gold auto-body paint, a greenhouse dining room, a domed kitchen, a corrugated aluminum "shed" studio, a grand stair topped by a black granite baldachino, and a corner clad in blue tile fish scales are not exactly the stuff of your average residential street, but no matter. Aided by a better-than-average budget, architect and client were able to design a fair amount of fantasy into the project— which doesn't mean, however, that it's all style and no substance. Gehry's rooftop village, outrageous as it looks from without, is elegantly proportioned within, and his generous use of glazing not only floods the interior with natural light, but offers a breathtaking, almost panoramic view of Los Angeles. As in the Aerospace Museum, the colliding exterior pieces enclose an interior that is continuous, expansive, and transparent enough to reveal several aspects of the outside at once from the inside. The simultaneous offering of visual richness and spatial simplicity is extremely appealing.

This was an unusual project for Gehry in that his client, Miriam Wosk, an artist with a strong decorative bent, worked closely with him on the design process and she designed all the interior tile work. Considering the difference in their respective sensibilities, the collaboration was all the more unusual, but the results seem to please both parties. Wosk's interiors and furnishings are fairly strong, but then so is Gehry's architecture; each one holds its own in what has turned out to be a positive tension. Where many architects would have felt threatened by

(opposite)
Sketch for Wosk
Residence 1982

ink on paper
10¾ x 8⅛
Collection the architect

outgrowth of the Smith House, which never was built.

The dome over the kitchen comes from Israel or that part of the world, and the curved stairway comes from many of the pictures that were shown to me of curved stairways. The use of marble and special tile was a strong client input. I invited the client to do some of the decor and participate in some of those considerations, so that when the building was finished it would be a collaboration. I thought we could each hold our own and be identified, and not hurt each other, not hurt each other's sensibility. That was the intent.

The client wanted a pink building, which threw me for a loop—and I think it threw the city of Beverly Hills for a loop—but somehow it all got absorbed and taken into consideration.

The budget here was considerably more than what I had been used to, so I was able to use some rather expensive materials. I didn't find that difficult. It was just different. I like the juxtaposition of cheaper materials against the richer ones. It's certainly an old idea. Louis Kahn did that years ago. I think that the step forms and the column form of the stairway and the collision of those forms at the living room is what I was after. Looking out the living room window, back toward the building, inward, you see the blue dome and the gold step form and the black granite. You see most of the elements and it creates an interesting landscape.

From inside you see the relationship of the fireplace to the high-rise towers of Century City. The pieces accrue to each other and by association make the outside more a part of the inside. I don't try to embellish anything, just show what's there. It's like Loyola, where we tried to accept the neighborhood, tried to make an inclusive strategy rather than an exclusive strategy. That idea is most successful in the Goldwyn library.

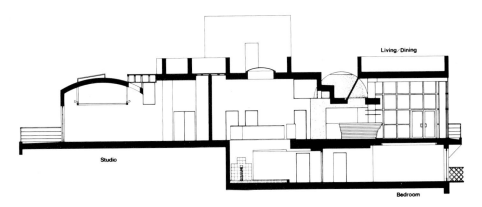

Section

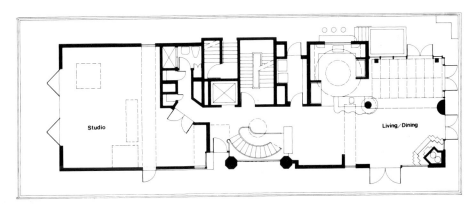

Upper Level Plan

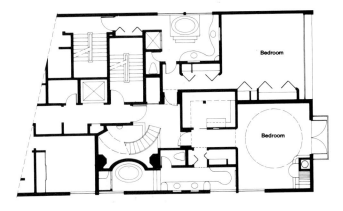

Lower Level Plan

180 — 181

Wosk Residence

(opposite, left)
The Wosk building prior to its renovation (top), and the completed remodeling (below) in which Gehry removed the top floor in order to create a new roofscape.

(opposite, right)
Wosk Residence elevations looking north (top) and south.

The Wosk Residence interiors reflect a complex mixture of client and architect attitudes. Yet Gehry achieved and retained a powerful layering of spaces and vistas amid the eclectic, hyperactive decor of the living-dining room.

such an arrangement, Gehry encouraged Wosk to develop her own aesthetic direction, whether or not it conformed to his own ideas.

A somewhat anomalous but nonetheless important project of the last few years is Gehry's design for the Temporary Contemporary (1983), the current home of The Museum of Contemporary Art in Los Angeles. A bare-bones renovation of two adjoining warehouses in the downtown Little Tokyo district, the project's nearly invisible budget of $1.2 million restricted Gehry to an absolute minimum number of architectural moves and he zeroed in on exactly the right ones. There was little room to play with three-dimensional forms: the only collision is that of the existing column grids of the two buildings, expressed by Gehry in the steel and chain-link canopy that he built over the street in front of the museum; and the only breaking up of forms occurs when the interior steel columns emerge from their code-required gypsumboard wrappings, at the point where the ceiling, if there were one, would be. But in spite of—or perhaps because of—its elegant austerity, the Temporary Contemporary has become something of a popular cause célèbre since its opening in 1983, by demonstrating that the same industrial buildings that have so long been used by artists as studios could be equally legitimate exhibition spaces for their work. MoCA asked Gehry to design the temporary museum after it had passed him over, in favor of Arata Isozaki, for the design of the permanent building. While their choice of Gehry might seem an almost Pavlovian reaction to the words "warehouse renovation," and while many architects of Gehry's stature would have flatly refused such a "consolation prize," there was, in fact, no more suitable architect for the job. Gehry's long-standing interest in contemporary art and artists, coupled with his innate sympathy for the low-budget effort, made this a project he couldn't refuse. When faced with the finished product, it is difficult to imagine that another architect could have created such comfortable exhibition space while preserving the inherent raw energy and beauty of the industrial buildings. Gehry once joked, "When people tell me that this is their favorite of all my projects, I know they like me best when I don't do too much." The Temporary Contemporary does offer tangible and widely-acclaimed proof of Gehry's uncanny knack for making the most of the least. Indeed, what may once have seemed to him a heartfelt defeat turned out to be a major victory.

In Gehry's most recent works—those designed since 1983—he continues to experiment with arrangements of architectural objects, but the nature of the objects themselves is starting to change. While this may be due in part to a finer tuning of Gehry's compositions, the forms, although they could hardly be any simpler, are somehow more highly resolved. Unfortunately, two of the most sophisticated projects from this period will not be built. Gehry's entry to the competition for the Médiathèque-Centre d'Art Contemporain in Nîmes, France (1984) is a dynamic synthesis of the forms and ideas expressed in his "collision"

A landmark in old Hollywood, the Danziger Studio-Residence is one of Gehry's first attempts to place various functions in discrete buildings on a single site—in this case a very small urban lot on a commercial street. Its asymmetrically arranged stucco cubes and clerestory windows provide privacy at the street and superb natural light in the double-height studio space.

Danziger Studio-Residence 1964
Hollywood, California

Lou Danziger, the well-known graphic designer, was one of the first clients willing to let us explore. There was a lot more freedom in this job than in those that had preceded it—and a lot more encouragement and support for ideas. The request for a separate studio and residence on the same lot led, quite naturally, to the two spaces. And since the connection had to be only at the ground floor, it led to this separation of two forms.

I was interested in doing a building that dealt with Melrose Avenue, a raunchy, commercial street. The complexity of the signage and the stuff on Melrose led me to try to make something simpler that would, by being recessive and quiet, stand on its own in that environment.

In an earlier project for Faith Plating I'd explored blown-on stucco, which at that time wasn't done very much, and we actually made full-scale mock-ups on Danziger and Faith Plating in an old garage in Venice, testing the equipment and exploring the texture. I was interested in using a natural cement color. We studied various colored cements and found there was a great variety from almost olive drab to light, whitish blue-gray. We chose the latter. The idea that he would never have to paint the building was important. So we started back then exploring materials more directly, and this was the product of that.

I was also concerned here with trying to get natural light in and the mix of warm light and cool light for an artist's studio. I objected to the all north-light studios, so I mixed the light at the back end and through the skylight, so it was not obtrusive, but it was mixed above eye level. The principles explored in the Danziger building reappear some years later in the Smith House.

The Temporary Contemporary 1983
The Museum of Contemporary Art
Los Angeles, California

The budget, as in most of our work, was absolutely rock bottom. There was remedial work on the old warehouse structure and seismic upgrading, lighting and electrical systems that took up seven-eighths of the budget. None of that would be seen as architecture. So the moves allowable were very few. The project wasn't treated lightly—it was treated with a great deal of care and seriousness. I didn't want to make any mistakes, for in a way I was competing with Arata Isozaki, who was designing the new Museum of Contemporary Art for the same client. The one bit of architecture that I allowed myself, the one move that was expensive was the canopy outside. I felt this was absolutely imperative since the future of that area foretold that the warehouses all around the Temporary Contemporary would be torn down shortly and that it would be left standing like a supermarket in a parking lot. With this early warning in mind, it became imperative to establish a territory, to give the building substance from the outside. That led to the canopy. The chain-link fencing as a canopy is a base for canvas tenting, which will enclose it and weatherproof it for certain outdoor functions. We would hope to have sculpture shows and things like that out there. And I had in mind also to cut a hole in the street, cut a wedge into the street and create a kind of amphitheater for a performance stage outside. That's never been done.

The enormous credit I've been getting for doing this has been wonderful, but we really did not do that much. We did sweep the floor and clean the skylights and steam clean the structure and ceiling rather than sandblast it, which I thought was important. We let the character of the old warehouse exist, tried not to change it and thus subordinate it, but rather to work within it to create a flexible space for contemporary art.

(opposite)
The Temporary Contemporary is entered beneath a chain-link canopy. A ramping system brings the visitor down into the galleries from the street level.

The Museum of Contemporary Art in Los Angeles, initially housed in this extraordinary warehouse remodeled by Gehry as a temporary site, has decided to retain this great exhibition space as a companion to the new, more formal building by Arata Isozaki. Large-scale works of contemporary art are beautifully shown in these vast spaces.

projects. But the elegant tautness and simplicity of the ziggurat that houses a contemporary art museum and libraries reveals Gehry at his most decisive and self-assured—too much so, perhaps, for the jury, which ultimately awarded the commission to another architect. One can't help feeling, however, that had it been built, this would have been one of Gehry's greatest works. Similarly, Camp Good Times, with its fanciful object-buildings strewn across an idyllic ocean-view site, would have given large-scale built form to one of Gehry's collaborations with artists—in this case, Claes Oldenburg and Coosje van Bruggen.

Nonetheless, these ideas continue to evolve in Gehry's new built works. The Sirmai-Peterson House, Thousand Oaks, California, is clearly related to the House for a Filmmaker, the Benson and Smith houses, in its breaking up of a 3,000 square-foot program into a number of discrete pieces. But while the parts of those earlier houses were arranged in no particular formal hierarchy, the components of this house are. The metal-clad cruciform building that houses the kitchen, dining room and den is the unmistakable focus and generating point of the composition, with its powerfully skewed axes "casting off" the smaller, clearly subordinate pieces that contain the two bedroom suites, which are reached by a bridge and a tunnel, respectively. While the composition as a whole is arranged to conform to the contours of the bucolic site, the tall tower that tops the cruciform building (consolidating ventilation stacks to create a clean roof line) is clearly visible from the path that leads down the ravine to the house.

While the Sirmai-Peterson House represents a further development of a now familiar theme, the Frances Howard Goldwyn Regional Branch Library strikes an entirely different note. The building, which occupies the downtown Hollywood site of a library that was destroyed by arson, is an asymmetrical composition. A tall central volume is flanked by reading rooms on the second floor and by twin water gardens just three feet below the second floor level, and is set back behind a nine-foot-high wall. It is hard to believe that the building, which looks positively imposing in model form, actually contains only 19,500 square feet. Gehry's skillful arrangement of forms on the tiny site makes the library seem much larger than it really is, while at the same time maintaining the scale of the low-rise commercial neighborhood around it. Gehry says that this building is "the closest to Classicism I've ever been," but this particular ode to Classicism is delivered in an updated-California-modern vocabulary. In this respect, the library actually bears a striking resemblance to Gehry's 1964 Danziger Studio, which is arguably one of his best buildings. Clad in palest green-enameled metal and peach stucco (colors that were made for southern California light), the cubic, transparent forms of the building and the light monitors that sit (asymmetrically) atop the reading-room "boxes" transcend the manufactured grandeur of downtown Hollywood without parodying it: the Library's elegant proportions and confident massing evoke genuine grandeur. In this building—which is public, although privately funded—Gehry has recaptured the awe-inspiring graciousness that has all but vanished from contemporary civic architecture. Its expansive, sun-washed reading rooms remind you of the days when a library was a place to read, rather than a warehouse in which to store books. And once again, the architect produced a major building on a shoestring budget of only three million dollars.

Finally, the most striking shift in Gehry's current work occurs in the design of the Winton Guest House in Wayzata, Minnesota. The guest house is built adjacent to, but separate from, the main house, a 1952 Philip Johnson design that was built for Mr. and Mrs. Richard C. Davis. Gehry's design, which started out in 1983 as a collection of objects, similar to that of the Sirmai-Peterson House, was transformed in 1985 into an arrangement of tiny buildings that are as close to pure sculpture as buildings can be. A garage clad in the Finnish plywood that was used on Loyola's chapel, a brick corner chimney form, a curved and vaulted stone building, and a shed covered in lead-coated copper all converge on a central tower/smokestack form, also in copper. The central tower and corner chimney forms offer a clear homage to Johnson's tiny library of 1980, which is located on his New Canaan, Connecticut estate—probably the modern movement's most famous collection of architectural objects in a landscape—a twentieth-century arcadian paradigm for Gehry's own experiments in this realm. But that same reductivist quality characterizes other parts of the Winton design as well. The vaulted stone building looks rather like an emerging fish form, and the wood-clad garage like a neatly-planed version of one of the logs in the log cabins that appear so often in Gehry's models. The almost mythical quality of these forms may come partly out of Gehry's recent collaborations with Claes Oldenburg, whose own transforma-tions of the most banal objects into larger-than-life monuments are not that far removed from Gehry's billboard-scaled chain-link curtains and jet-plane logos; but their sculptural clarity points more directly to another of Gehry's inspirations, the images of Brancusi's studio. Pro-cess, however, is nowhere in sight here: the arrangements of forms in the Winton project appear effortless. Like the perfect crime, there are no signs of a struggle, and no trace of the murder weapon.

Whether or not this signals a major change in Gehry's work remains to be seen. No matter how far his buildings push the limits of architec-ture toward those of sculpture, they remain, above all, buildings. His large-scale projects have made a significant impact on the loosely-woven urban fabric of Los Angeles. How Gehry's singular vision will affect the more tightly-woven, older and more fragile fabric of East Coast and European cities is a question whose answer we await as eagerly as Gehry awaits the chance to answer it.

**Frances Howard Goldwyn
Regional Branch Library   1983-1986
Hollywood, California**

The Hollywood library was a commission from
Samuel Goldwyn, Jr., who donated money to
the city of Los Angeles to build a library
bearing his mother's name, Frances Howard
Goldwyn. His only stipulation was that our
office be retained to design the building. Mr.
Goldwyn's wishes were very modest in terms
of program. He wanted a building that his
mother would have been proud of, and
something that would be appropriately
dignified for the kind of facility it was and for
the kind of person she was.

The original library on this site had been
something of a mecca for film writers and
people doing research for movies. The original
building was burned down and the arsonist
was never found, so the city of Los Angeles
was very paranoid about that. They said that
we had to pay attention to security. The
security requirements were more stringent
here than they were for the embassy I once
tried to design in Damascus. The city librarian
said that if he had his way we'd have
twenty-foot walls around the building, a moat
and piranha fish.

(top)
Looking west from the street
opposite the entry, the
library's cubistic reading
room enclosures create a
fascinating asymmetrical
facade.

The library's steel-framed
structure has a stucco and
sheet metal exterior.

The visitor steps down from
the sidewalk to the entry
level below. A steel gate
encloses the entrance stair.

The library is entered down a short stairway from the sidewalk on the east street side.

Frances Howard Goldwyn Regional Branch Library

The north reading room.

Frances Howard Goldwyn Regional Branch Library

A second floor glass-enclosed light well is surrounded by the children's reading room.

(right)
A seating area of colorful ceramic tile in the north reading room provides a quiet spot from which to contemplate the reflecting pool.

I was concerned about fitting this building into its surroundings, making it an inclusive object and making the pieces around it seem part of the composition. I started out with a symmetrical, classical arrangement in which you enter in a court and go down the middle, with reading rooms left and right, backed up to the stacks. As we progressed, the reading rooms were placed in a water garden behind a wall. The torquing away from symmetry and formalism occurred naturally in response to the sun. When I started opening up the north walls and closing the south walls, this led to an asymmetrical arrangement in which the southern-most reading room looked at a solid wall, the main hall looked through glass toward the northern-most reading room—an object sitting in space—and the northern-most reading room looked at Hollywood. So each room takes on a unique character.

The cube of the north reading room is seen through the window of the children's library.

Frances Howard Goldwyn Regional Branch Library

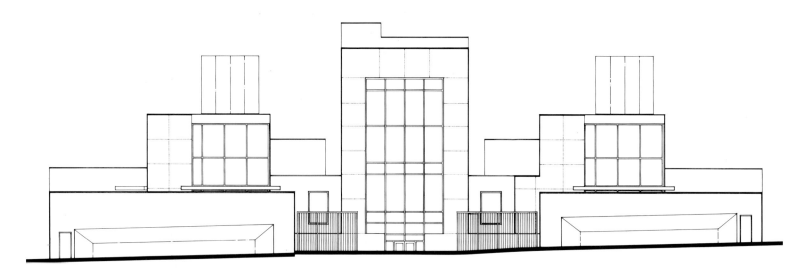

East Facade

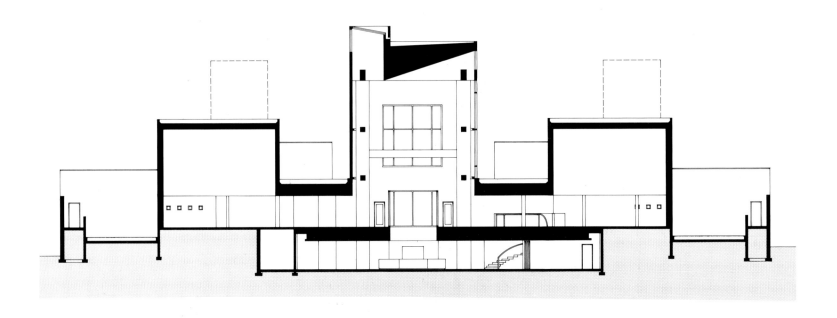

North-South Section

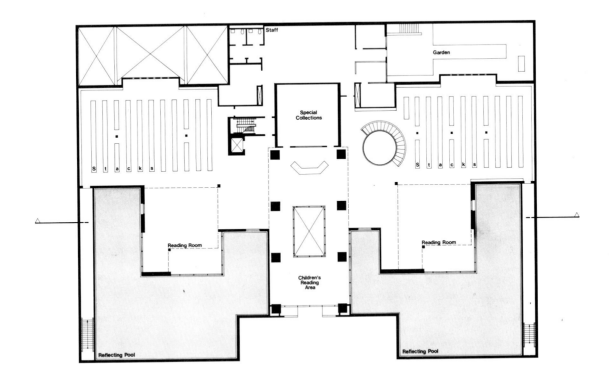

Second Floor

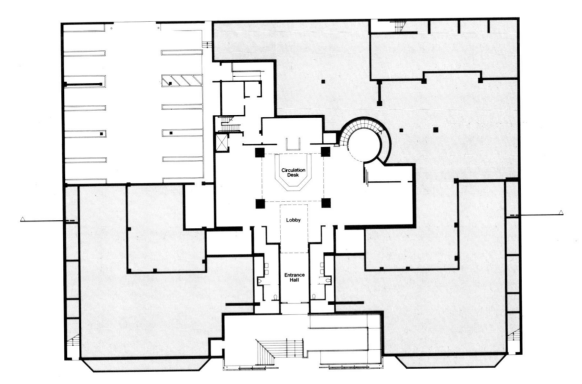

First Floor

Sirmai-Peterson House   1984-1986
Thousand Oaks, California

An aerial view of the
Sirmai-Peterson model
describes the relationships
of the buildings to the

courtyard that preoccupied
Gehry in this design.

(left)
Views of the model looking south (top) and east.

(from top)
These views of the model, looking north and southeast from the interior courtyard,

demonstrate the ways in which the architect has taken advantage of the site's varied topography.

Beautiful site—two acres adjacent to a ravine and a storm drain. This was a technical problem that had to be dealt with, and it suggested damming and making a small lake. I wanted the building to sit as close to the ravine as possible, because it was in the middle of the site and had the potential of commanding the site in a variety of ways so that each part of the house could have its own character.

The clients kidded me about my previous work in which every room was a separate building and said they really liked the Ron Davis Studio which had one big space. We had a lot of fun. Every time they came into the office I would have a new building. These people are among the most supportive clients we've had.

Sirmai-Peterson House

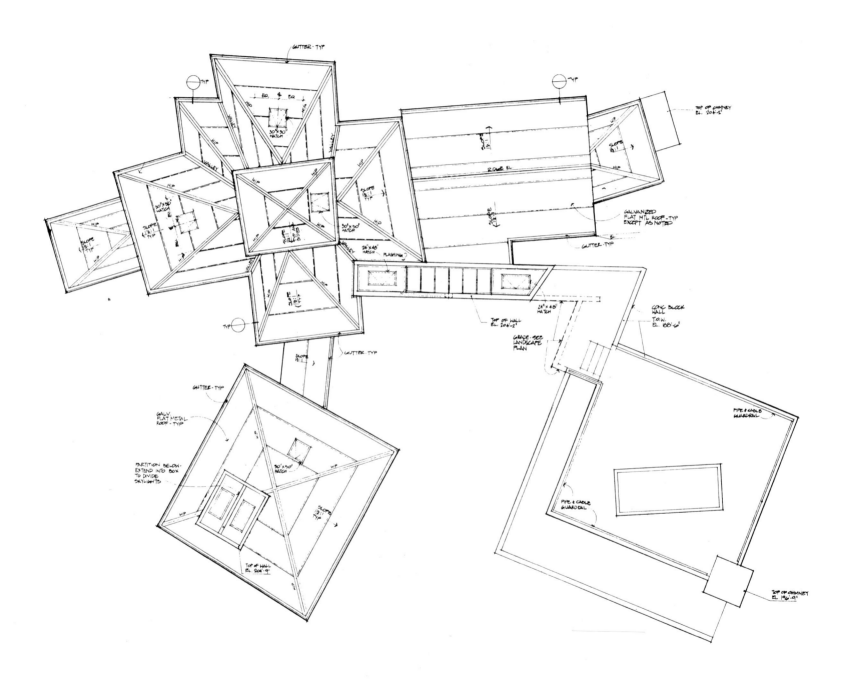

Roof Plan

The final design for the house happened when I was on vacation in Panama, spending a couple of weeks with my wife's family. Everybody's very Catholic. I don't know if this had anything to do with the churchlike form of this house—but the Petersons seem to think it did. I've spent a good deal of time studying Romanesque churches, and I see some of that coming out here. We started with a centralized church plan, where the kitchen, dining room, entry and den cross, and then we added a nave for the living room and an apse for the fireplace and a side aisle as the hall that takes you down to the living room and to the bedrooms. It wasn't a conscious church plan, but lining up the pieces along the edge led to that kind of resolution.

In this house we are putting the objects back together, trying to make an architectural vocabulary. It's logical to play with disparate sizes and put them together; in this house that happens in an interesting way. The pieces still collide, but it's more continous here than in earlier houses. It's a more traditional spatial experience. If you look at the whole thing as the exploration of a vocabulary—starting with the simplest thing, and then embellishing—it becomes more and more complex. Now I'm working on a couple of houses that have only one material, getting back to quite a conventional scenario, but with a new way of looking at it for me. I'm going around the barn door to get to some other kind of iteration of the standard house, which has all one material and is spatially integrated and organized.

The Sirmai-Peterson House has one interesting thing that I haven't done before: the formal space between the bedrooms and the living room. It's a monumental residential space, that courtyard in between. You see it when you come into the entry, and you get to it from the living room and from the bedroom. I think that space is like the center of town in a medieval city. It reminds me of that anyway. I've created a town square for this house, and I think it's going to work like that. All the other rooms face out toward the lake and toward the ravine. I can't wait until it is finished.

Sketches for Sirmai-Peterson House   1984
ink on paper
11 x 14 each
Collection the architect

Early sketches of the Sirmai-Peterson House, particularly the site plan, are remarkably like the finished plan. Gehry has an inspired way of "getting it right" from the start, although every project is taken through a long evolution of studied modifications.

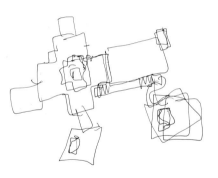

Winton Guest House   1983-1986
Wayzata, Minnesota

In this small, but major, work Gehry has explored a variety of solutions through a series of study models. The early versions are illustrated on this page and opposite. The final version follows.

The 1952 Philip Johnson house (top) sits at the top of the site that slopes gently down toward Lake Minnetonka.

In the earliest models, vestiges of the Benson House (pp 118-121) are visible in the placement and suggested materials of the elements.

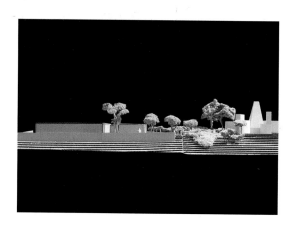

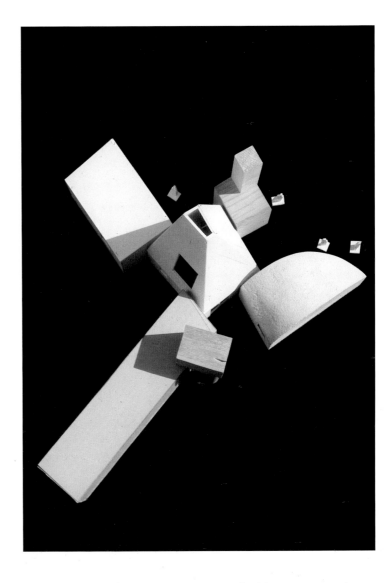

The Wintons are art collectors with a very strong commitment to contemporary art. They live in a Philip Johnson house that was designed in the early fifties and they needed to build a guest house. So they did the logical thing, but Philip turned them down. There was a concern that building a house of a different style would look like somebody was subdividing this wonderful estate, and it would somehow be a denigration of its

character. I think that was a valid concern. We tried to stay away from the Philip Johnson house. I didn't want to mess around with Uncle Philip's baby. I'm sure he was horrified when he heard I was doing it. So I decided to go on the other side of the hedge where we could create a separate zone. But the guest house as it's finally designed is inviting us to take the hedge down.

On this page we see the beginning of the metamorphosis that led to the final images (overleaf). Although this is a cruciform plan, each arm is unique.

Winton Guest House

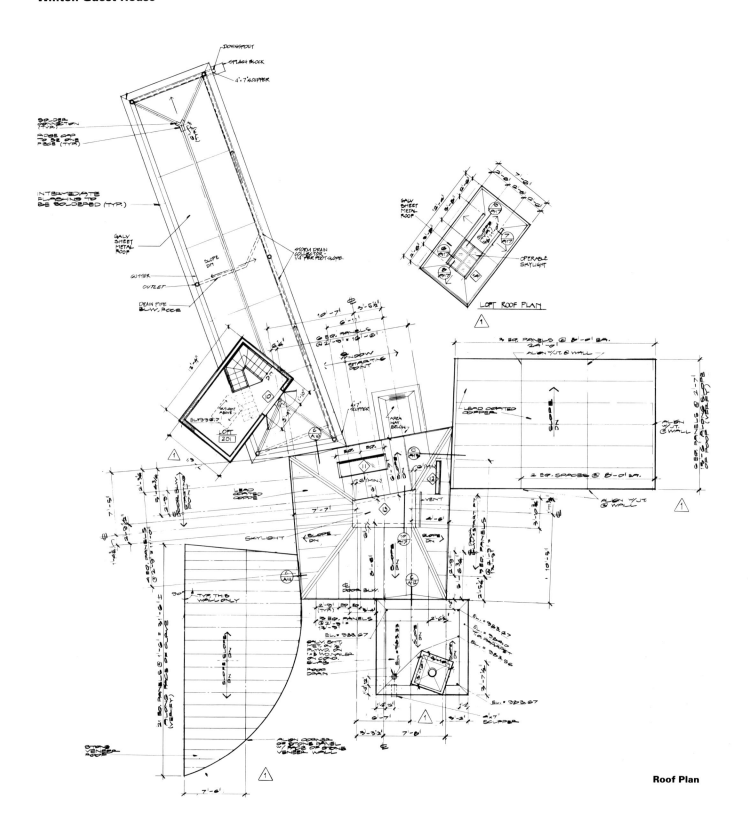

LOFT ROOF PLAN

Roof Plan

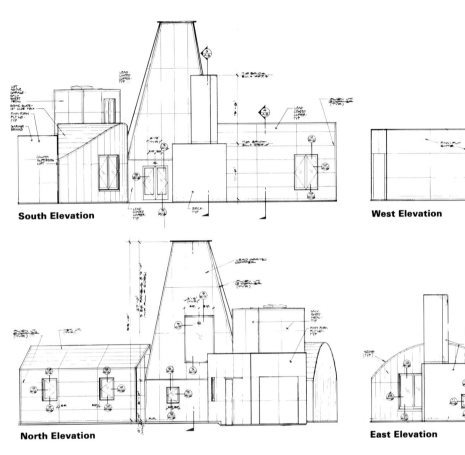

South Elevation

West Elevation

North Elevation

East Elevation

What slowly evolved is a very sculptural solution that may be construed as a large, outdoor sculpture. When it's seen from the Philip Johnson house it won't look as much like a building as like a large sculpture. The parts of the house are very simple forms. They're put together in a way similar to the Smith House and earlier projects. Here I had the opportunity to go higher with some, unlike the other places. The earlier houses, like Wosk and Smith, had height limitations. They tended to make one level. Here, as in the Sirmai-Peterson House, I had the ability to go higher. So we made a central living room that is towerlike. This building is very tiny. It doesn't have a tight budget—it has a very adequate budget—so we're cladding the

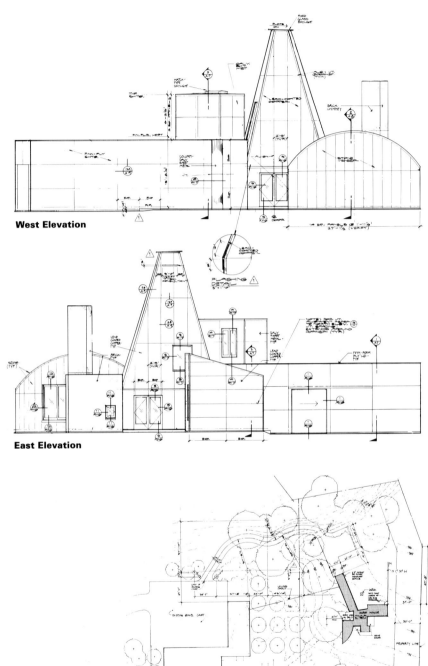

↑
N

Site Plan

Winton Guest House

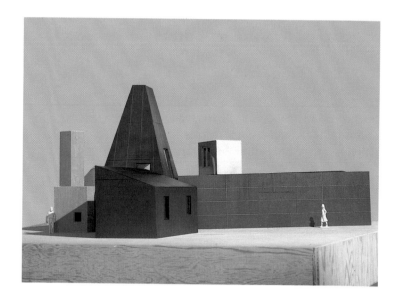

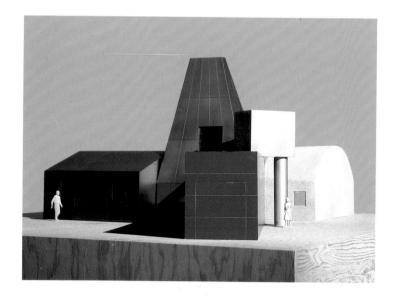

pieces in lead-coated copper and stone, and in Finnish plywood, one of my favorites, the same material I used on the Loyola chapel. And there's some brick in the fireplace.

The pieces are placed together in a tight complex, like a still life, like a Morandi. The breakthrough for me in this house was the idea of cracks between the buildings, wedge-shaped cracks that serve to differentiate the parts of the pure forms and suggest that they are complete forms because of this cleavage. But in Minnesota one can imagine having snow and ice get into the cracks and that would be very difficult. We started with a very convoluted, elaborate scheme to get the water out, which seemed unnecessarily complex. Finally, when we built large-scale models we could see that the saddle detail that one would use on a normal roof was of a reasonable scale so that it would not be visible, and the crack, the wedge, could still be maintained. That was one consideration. The other consideration was future expansion.

The Wintons have high hopes of having many grandchildren, as their five children are

starting to produce families. So it is hoped that this building will have a certain amount of humor and mystery and fantasy, so that visiting children will remember their trip to grandma's house. There are places to hide and crawl into and there will be spaces added in the future.

Frank O. Gehry and Associates Staff 1962-1986

Xavier Aboitiz
Katrin Adams
Margo Alofsin
Roberta Altoon
Ronald Altoon
Laurie Anderson
Michele Andrew
Marc Appleton
Mary Armstrong
Diane Arnold
Michael Asher
Romeo Asprec
Alan Au
Gerhard Auernhammer
Vaughn Babcock
Adelino Bacani
Fred Ballard
Madeline Banchik
George Barnes
Larry Barrish
Robert Beauchamp
Peter Becker
Patricia Belton-Oliver
Jeffrey Bernstein
Robert Bernstein
Richard Berry
Rebecca Berwick
Sarah Berwick
Aaron Betsky
Wesley Bilson
Perry Blake
Thomas Blaskiewitz
William Block
Donald Bloom
Joan Bonner
Albert Borgo
Marla Brasius
Nancy Braswell
David Brodsley
Tom Buresh
Wilfredo Burgas
Donald Burton
Pamela Burton
Donald Carlson
Claudia Carol
Joshua Chaiken
Edwin Chan
Yuk Chan
William Chapman
John Chase
Gerald Chavez

Virginia Chesman
Anna Chin
Ildiko Choy
Dona Christianson
John Clagett
Timothy Clement
Gregory Cloud
Robert Cloud
Suzanne Coles
James Collimore
Kathleen Connell
William Cooperman
Jesus Corpus
Renato Corzo
Joyce Cox
Clodualdo Crisostomo
Miguel Cruchaga
Jerzy Czerwinski
Stephen Dane
Jeffrey Daniels
John Dash
William Daughlash
Carlton Davis
Douglas Davis
John Davis
Christopher Dawson
Gabrielle de Ganges
Jean de Gastines
David Denton
Charles Dilworth
Penny Dolginer
Pamela Donnelly
Elizabeth Doore
Jan Dorbritz
Robert Doyle
Douglas Dworsky
Sheri Eaton
Davood Ebtekar
Addison Edwards
Nicholas Eisenman
Alan Erenberg
Ian Espinoza
Brett Ettinger
Veronica Felder
Gary Ferguson
Jesse Ferguson
Frederick Fisher
Michael Folonis
Valerie Fong
Robert Ford
Kenneth Francis

Irene Frankel
Kathryn Frankel
Matthew Fry
Douglas Gagan
Ignacio Garcia
John Garritson
Elizabeth Gaskins
Berta Gehry
Brina Gehry
Frank Gehry
Leslie Gehry
Thelma Gehry
Ralph Gentile
Andra Georges
Jaime Gesundheit
Fereydoon Ghaffari
James Gibbs
Diane Gillis
Arnold Ginsberg
Katherine Goff
Gary Goldsmith
Elyse Grinstein
Anne Hale
Robert Hale
Carol Han
Carla Harary
Stephen Harger
Michael Hargrave
Helen Harris
David Hertz
Ruth Higley
Roy Holman
Ann Hosfeld
Paula Howard
Gary Hulton
James Hutton
Douglas Hyun
Tahn Hyun
Rene Ilustre
Alfredo Javier
Ronald Johnson
John Johnston
Joanne Joyce
Ramon Juncal
Gerald Kamitaki
Daniel Kantor
Gere Kavanaugh
Mark Keiserman
David Kellen
Kiki Keyser
Reynold Kimura

Donald King
Lynda King
Ramon Klein
Gerald Komity
Jerry Kotas
Paul Krueger
Mitzi Kubrick
Eugene Kupper
Heather Kurze
Kenneth Kuss
Amy Lann
Matthew Larrabee
Myriam Laverde
Mitchell Lawrence
Michael Lehrer
Jeffrey Lentz
William Lester
Beni Leutenegger
Edward Levine
Dale Lewis
Ernesto Leyva
Paul Lintz
Charles Lowry
Paul Lubowicki
Jose Luciano
Richard Luke
Maynard Lyndon
Dominique Lyon
Brian Maridan
Robert Maxwell
Alex Meconi
Beverly Meredith
Nancy Michali
Thomas Michali
Erica Millar
Steven Millington
Marjorie Mix
Mitzi Montgomery
Michael Moran
John Morgan
Robert Moriarty
Paul Nagashima
Susan Nardulli
Enrique Navarrete
John New
John Newman
Shirley Nounan
Charles Oakley
Thomas Ochi
Ruben Ojeda
Jean O'Laire

Eamonn O'Mahony
David O'Malley
Adolpho Ortega
Richard Orne
Ewa Osinski
Tomasz Osinski
Patricia Owen
Charles Patton
Sharon Peckinpah
Dean Perton
Barton Phelps
Anthony Pleskow
Claire Pollock
Jerry Pomerantz
Albert Pope
Stephen Porten
James Porter
Paul Prejza
Undine Prohl
Jerry Radin
David Reyes
Melchor Reyes
Ralph Ridgeway
Loriah Robinson
Antonio Rodriguez
Virgilio Rodriguez
Antonio Romano
Frank Romero
David Rosen
Ricardo Sabella
Joan Sacks
Edwin Sankey
Joan Santagata
Richardo Santiano
Brent Saville
Marna Schnabel
David Schneider
Molly Schneider
Stephen Schuck
Frederick Schwartz
Mark Schwartz
Josh Schweitzer
Hak Sik Son
Sandi Simola
Sharon Singer
Jerry Sirlin
Alexis Smith
Richard Smith
Richard Snyder
Elsie Solvberg
Katherine Spitz

John Staff
Allan Stanton
Allison Stern
Carroll Stockard
Deborah Sussman
Radoslav Sutnar
Donald Swiers
Naomi Swiers
Tim Swischuk
Maureen Tamuri
Ernest Tanji
Chitra Techaphaibul
George Terpatsi
Bryce Thomas
Morgan Thomas
Steven Tomko
Alan Tossman
Tziporah Toubi
Joseph Toussaint
Elliot Tsujiuchi
Bruce Tucker
Clay Tudor
Wayne Twedell
Frederick Usher
Roderick Usher
Rachel Vert
Mark Wagner
Kin Wah Yung
Robert Walder
Kenneth Walker
Gregory Walsh
Margaret Watson
Laurie Weeks

Authors' Biographies

Rosemarie Haag Bletter

Rosemarie Haag Bletter is Adjunct Associate Professor, Institute of Fine Arts, New York University. She is the author of several books, including *Skyscraper Style-Art Deco New York* (with Cervin Robinson), and she was a guest curator for the Whitney Museum of American Art's recent exhibition, *High Styles: Twentieth-Century American Design,* as well as one of the authors of the exhibition catalogue.

Coosje van Bruggen

Art historian Coosje van Bruggen has collaborated on large-scale projects with her husband, artist Claes Oldenburg, and Frank Gehry. She has been a guest curator for the Stedelijk Museum, Amsterdam, and the Kunstmuseum Basel.

Henry N. Cobb

A founding member of I.M. Pei and Partners, Henry N. Cobb has been a principal architect in the firm since 1955. Together with an active architectural practice, Cobb is also a renowned teacher and from 1980 to 1985 he served as Chairman of the Department of Architecture at the Harvard Graduate School of Design. His major recent works include the Portland Museum of Art in Maine, and Commerce Square in Philadelphia.

Mildred Friedman

As Design Curator at Walker Art Center, Mildred Friedman is the organizer of the exhibition *The Architecture of Frank Gehry* and editor of *Design Quarterly* magazine. She organized the 1981 exhibition *De Stijl: 1917-1931, Visions of Utopia* and was co-curator of *Tokyo: Form and Spirit*, 1986.

Joseph Giovannini

A writer on architecture and design based in New York City, Joseph Giovannini has contributed to such architectural journals as *Skyline, Metropolis* and *Architectural Digest.* From Los Angeles, he was active in the architectural community there, writing as architecture critic for the *Los Angeles Herald Examiner.*

Thomas S. Hines

Thomas S. Hines is Professor of the History of Architecture, University of California, Los Angeles. He was a 1984-1985 recipient of a Fulbright Fellowship to the University of Exeter, and he has written extensively on the work of Daniel Burnham, Richard Neutra and Frank Lloyd Wright.

Pilar Viladas

After serving as managing editor of *Skyline* and special features editor at *Interiors,* Pilar Viladas joined the staff of *Progressive Architecture* magazine, where she is a senior editor.

Lenders to
the Exhibition

Armand Bartos
Keith Berwick
Jay Chiat
Lucinda Childs
Deborah Doyle
Berta Gehry
Frank Gehry
Joseph Giovannini
Fred Hoffman
Kady Hoffman
Mr. and Mrs. Robert Meltzer
Montifiore Foundation, New York
The Museum of Modern Art, New York
Doreen Nelson
New City Editions, Venice, California
City of Nîmes, France
Claes Oldenburg and Coosje van Bruggen
Joan and Jack Quinn
San Francisco Museum of Modern Art
Penny and Mike Winton

Acknowledgments

Going to California for the past three years to work with Frank Gehry has given me the opportunity to revisit familiar old neighborhoods and to discover new ones that did not exist when I was young in Los Angeles. In this period I've come to recognize the significance of Gehry's role in the evolution of that city's architecture and to consider his place in the international scene.

In his Los Angeles work, Gehry is always mindful of history and context without being archaistic. Aware of existing forms, he nevertheless insists on looking ahead, on inventing. Consequently, he has assumed the mantle of earlier California form-givers: Greene and Greene, Frank Lloyd Wright, Rudolph Schindler and Richard Neutra. But, perhaps because of his training as a planner, he has been especially conscious of those quintessential characteristics that are Los Angeles: the boxlike assemblage of the Spanish bungalow, the textures of stucco and tile, the unique shape of a desert cactus, and most important to his aesthetic, the quality of western light that creates the region's sunbaked colors and long, cool shadows.

What Gehry has accomplished in Los Angeles is increasingly influential elsewhere, and as he goes on to build in other American cities and abroad, his versatility and sensitivity to place will undoubtedly allow him to transform other environments as he has that ,of southern California. So my first thanks are to Gehry, the architect.

This exhibition could not have been organized without the assistance of Eamonn O'Mahony, of Frank O. Gehry and Associates. He has gathered the essential materials for our history of Gehry's work, both written and photographic, and his advice in many areas has been invaluable. Assistance with the essays in this book has come from a number of people, but I would particularly like to acknowledge that of Greg Walsh, a longtime associate of Gehry's, who provided an oral history of the architect's exhibition designs. The choreographer Lucinda Childs wrote a detailed description of her collaboration with Gehry in a letter to me, as did Stephanie

Barron, Curator, Twentieth-Century Art at the Los Angeles County Museum of Art, who has worked on several exhibition installations with the architect. Ernest Fleischmann, the Executive Director of the Los Angeles Philharmonic Association and General Director of the Hollywood Bowl, participated in a lively, extended telephone interview in which he outlined the history of the Bowl for me. Special thanks are due Claes Oldenburg who has given us permission to reproduce a number of his drawings in this book that relate to projects he has undertaken with Gehry. And the authors—Rosemarie Haag Bletter, Coosje van Bruggen, Henry N. Cobb, Joseph Giovannini, Thomas S. Hines, and Pilar Viladas—have earned our admiration for their analyses and insights into many aspects of the architect's life and work.

We are extremely grateful for the loans of furniture, lamps and drawings that have come from a number of lenders who are acknowledged at left. Particular thanks are owed Fred Hoffman, director of New City Editions, who has been helpful in locating objects and securing loans for the exhibition.

I'm grateful to the members of the Walker Art Center staff who have worked with me in the preparation of this book and the exhibition it accompanies. Their names are given on page 216. I want particularly to thank Lorraine Ferguson, the Art Center's graphic designer, who spent many hours creating the design of this book.

My final thanks are to Berta and Frank Gehry for their generous hospitality and friendship throughout the development of this book and the exhibition it documents.

Mildred Friedman

Bibliography

A definitive bibliography through January 1985 may be found in *Frank Gehry, Buildings and Projects,* compiled and edited by Peter Arnell and Ted Bickford (New York: Rizzoli, 1985), a catalogue raisonné of the projects of Frank O. Gehry and Associates to that date. The listing below includes material published since February 1985.

Books

Macrae-Gibson, Gavin. *The Secret Life of Buildings: An American Mythology for Modern Architecture.* Cambridge, MA: The MIT Press, 1986, pp 2-29.

Marder, Tod A., ed., *The Critical Edge, Controversy in Recent American Architecture.* Cambridge, MA: The MIT Press, 1985, pp 101-112.

Periodicals

"Wosk Residence," *GA Houses 17,* February 1985.

Rabeneck, Andrew. "Positive Space: The California Aerospace Museum," *Arts and Architecture,* Volume 3, Number 4, 1985.

Viladas, Pilar. "Form Follows Ferment," *Progressive Architecture,* February 1985.

Anargyros, Sophie and de Valdivia, Marco. "Espace Brut," *Decoration Internationale,* February 1985.

Stambler, Lyndon. "Developer Dreams of Art Museum in Egg-Packing Plant," *Los Angeles Times,* 17 February 1985.

Gregotti, Vittorio. "Un messaggio dalla California," *Panorama,* 17 February 1985.

Anderson, Alexandra. "Gehry's Fish," *Architectures,* Winter 1985.

Jones, Alan. "L.A.'s Temporary Contemporary," *Architectures,* Winter 1985.

Ianco-Starrls. "Loyola Law School to Celebrate New Campus," *Los Angeles Times,* 17 March 1985.

Knight III, Carleton. "Philip Johnson," *The Christian Science Monitor,* 21 March 1985.

Fulton, William. "Loyola Law School Bears Gehry's Mark," *Evening Outlook,* 29 March 1985.

Kaplan, Sam Hall. "Philip Johnson: Architecture's Icon," *Los Angeles Times,* 31 March 1985.

"Les Jeux de Cubes de Frank Gehry," *Actuel,* April 1985.

Fulton, William. "Architect's Playful Hand Seen in Loyola's New Campus," *The Los Angeles Daily Journal,* 1 April 1985.

"U.S. stars to talk in London," *Building Design,* 5 April 1985.

Muchnic, Suzanne. "Spiritual Eye Lost at Loyola Law School," *Loyola Law School,* 9 April 1985.

Bramen, Robert. "Architectural Training: Six Metro Rail Stations," *L.A. Architect,* April 1985.

Gandee, Charles K. "Norton House, Venice, California," *Architectural Record,* Mid-April 1985.

Russell, John. "'Temporary Contemporary' offers a sample of Museum's Grand Design," *International Herald Tribune,* 13,14 April 1985.

Kaplan, Sam Hall. "The Roses and Lemons of Downtown L.A.," *Los Angeles Times,* 3 May 1985.

Dunlop, Beth. "Architects accept the challenge: Turn mundane into the sublime," *The Miami Herald,* 5 May 1985.

Pastier, John. "Distillation of a Paradoxical City," *Architecture,* May 1985.

Rey, Roberto Rocca. "Architettura Domani," *IL PIA CERE* (Milano), May 1985.

Zevi, Bruno. "Libero di volare," *L'Espresso,* May 1985.

Jenkins, John A. "Is This Any Way to Sell a Computer?" *Ambassador* (TWA Magazine), May 1985.

"Cross Currents of American Architecture," *Architectural Design 55,* No. 1/2, 1985.

Jencks, Charles. "Frank Gehry—The Deconstructionist," *Art & Design,* May 1985.

Schiro, Anne-Marie. "Transforming a Manhattan Carriage House," *The New York Times,* 30 May 1985.

"Atlantic Crossing," *Building Design,* 24 May 1985.

Goldberger, Paul. "Architecture: Impact of Buildings on Society," *The New York Times,* 31 May 1985.

Lyon, Domenique. "Frank O. Gehry: Avis de tempete surle Pacifique," *L'Architecture d'Aujourd' hui,* June 1985.

"Frank O. Gehry and Associates, Inc.," *Architecture in Greece 19,* 1985.

Celant, Germano. "Frank O. Gehry and Associates, Loyola Law School e Aerospace Museum a Los Angeles," *Casabella,* June 1985.

"Us and Them," *Building Design,* 7 June 1985.

"Some Talk of Alexander," *Building Design,* 14 June 1985.

Rabinovich, Abraham. "Talmudic Influence," *The Jerusalem Post,* 12 July 1985.

Gapp, Paul. "Who says Witty can't be serious?" *Chicago Tribune,* 21 July 1985.

Rico, Diana. "In Search of L.A.'s ugliest buildings," *Daily News,* 27 July 1985.

Rico, Diana. "American Architecture," *Daily News,* 27 July 1985.

"The Fifties: Re-Living it up—Manhattan Moderne," *Life,* August 1985.

Citron, Alan. "Proposed $16 million Venice Complex seen as Both Boon, Burden," *Los Angeles Times,* 4 August 1985.

Kaplan, Sam Hall. "Critical Edge Enters Architectural Debate," *Los Angeles Times,* 9 August 1985.

"Langes Messer fahrt durch Venedig," *Der Spiegel,* 19 August 1985.

"Frank Gehry est les boites," *Construction Moderne,* September 1985.

Katkov, Richard. "The Wosk House," *L.A. Architect,* September 1985.

Vincitorio, Francesco. "Oldenburg, un campiello pieno di Vip," *LA STAMPA,* 7 September 1985.

Drohojowska, Hunter. "A View From The Top," *Los Angeles Herald Examiner,* 15 September 1985.

Slesin, Suzanne. "Tracing the Paths of 20th-Century American Design," *The New York Times,* 19 September 1985.

"Clemi 1985 Design Award," *World Fence News,* October 1985.

"A Century of American Design," *Northwest Orient,* October 1985.

Kaplan, Sam Hall. "Trendy Projects Win Most AIA Awards," *Los Angeles Times,* 13 October 1985.

Glueck, Grace. "Conceptual Art, Italian Style, Makes a Statement at P.S.I," *The New York Times,* 13 October 1985.

Hoag, Paul Sterling. "Critical Edge," *L.A. Architect,* October 1985.

Knight III, Carleton. "Frank Gehry, in Houston," *Leading Edge,* October 1985.

Iden, Peter. "Ausflug in die kalifornische Spatantike," *Samstag,* 19 October 1985.

Binosi, Remo. "Oldenburg: Oggetti al Potere," *Grazia,* 20 October 1985.

Jencks, Charles. "House on a Hot Pink Roof," *House & Garden,* November 1985.

Reid, David. "California: The New Alexandria," *Vanity Fair,* November 1985.

"LA/AIA Design Awards," *L.A. Architect,* November 1985.

"Una Casa Che Non Si Fa Inghiottire," *Abitare 238,* October 1985.

Goldberger, Paul. "Modernism Reaffirms Its Power," *The New York Times,* 24 November 1985.

Spoor, Andre. "Steen Des Aanstoots," *Handelsbad,* November 1985.

Viladas, Pilar. "Rooms at the Top," *Progressive Architecture,* December 1985.

Muschamp, Herbert. "Ground Up," *Artforum,* December 1985.

Fumagalli, Paolo. "Geschichte (n) furdie Gegenwart," *Werk, Bauen & Wohnen,* December 1985.

Goldberger, Paul. "Architecture," *The New York Times,* December 1985.

Kaplan, Sam Hall. "Low-Rise Profile of High-Rise Architect," *Los Angeles Times,* 20 December 1985.

Anderson, Kurt. "The Shape of Things to Come," *Time,* 23 December 1985.

"Leon Whiteson: Architecture," *Los Angeles Herald Examiner,* 29 December 1985.

Goldberger, Paul. "Frank O. Gehry: Aerospace, Loyola and Norton," *Architecture and Urbanism,* January 1986.

Andersen, Kurt. "Breaking Out of the Box," *Time,* 6 January 1986.

Kornbluth, Jesse. "Journey through Space," *House & Garden,* February 1986.

Kisselgoff, Anna. "Choreography Swamped by Decor," *The New York Times,* 9 February 1986.

Index

(Page numbers in bold-face type indicate illustrations.)

Photo Credits

Morley Baer
pp 22, 23

Fred Ballard
pp 130 (left), 136, 137

D. James Dee
p 81 (bottom)

Frank O. Gehry
p 150 (top)

Hans Hammarsklöld,
courtesy Claes Oldenburg
p 10

Larry Harris p 81 (top)

T. Kitajima
pp 26, 27, 34, 35,
38 (left and lower right),
42, 43 (right)

Robert Lautman
pp 72, 73

Richard N. Levine
p 105 (bottom)

Michael Moran
cover, frontispiece, pp 21, 62, 68,
69, 70, 78, 106, 107, 111, 118, 119,
146, 150 (bottom), 151, 154, 155,
156, 157, 158, 162, 163, 166, 167,
170, 171, 174, 175, 178, 179, 182,
183, 185, 189, 190-197, 198, 199, 202
(left and top), 203 (left)

Grant Mudford
pp 86, 186 (top)

Courtesy The Museum of
Modern Art, New York
pp 47, 69 (top)

Eamonn O'Mahony
pp 71, 109, 116, 117, 135, 138, 139,
142, 143, 152, 153, 202 (bottom
right), 203 (right), 206, 207

Eric Politzer
pp 122, 131

Marvin Rand
pp 20, 66, 88, 89, 90, 91, 105 (center)

Jack Ross
p 65

Otto Rothschild
p 105 (top)

Mark Schwartz
pp 50, 51, 54, 55

Courtesy Sprengel Museum,
Hannover
p 47

Ezra Stoller Associates,
courtesy Philip Johnson
p 202

Tim Street-Porter
pp 15, 25, 30, 31, 38, (top right), 39,
43 (left), 56, 61, 74, 82, 83, 84, 85,
92-96, 98, 99, 114, 115, 147 (top left),
186 (bottom), 187

Steve Tomko
pp 100

Clay Tudor
pp 58, 59

Tom Vinetz
pp 103, 147 (lower left and right)

Dorothy Zeidman
p 127